Woman at Work

Woman at Work

The autobiography of
MARY ANDERSON as told to
MARY N. WINSLOW

Minneapolis 1951
THE UNIVERSITY OF MINNESOTA PRESS
LONDON · GEOFFREY CUMBERLEGE · OXFORD UNIVERSITY PRESS

PRINTED AT THE LUND PRESS, INC., MINNEAPOLIS

We come from many lands,
We march for very far;
In hearts and lips and hands
Our staff and weapons are.
The light we walk in darkens
Sun and moon and star.

SWINBURNE

Foreword

WHEN Mary Anderson and I embarked on the project of compiling a record of her life and work, there were several alternatives open to us. We could make it a careful study of certain phases of the development of women's participation in the organized labor movement and in industrial employment, but others more competent than we had already produced masses of reports on these subjects. We could make it an account of the dramatic progress of an immigrant girl from an ill-paid job as a domestic servant to a position of importance in the government of the United States, but hundreds of newspapers and magazines had already done this. We could make it the human story of a woman, showing what influenced her life and her character, and the part she played in the great movements of her time. This we have tried to do. The story is strictly autobiographical. It has been filtered but not embroidered. It is in Mary Anderson's own words, stenographically recorded during hours of conversation and interviews. Interpretations and editorial comment have been purposely omitted in the belief that the personality and quality of the author will emerge most clearly through her own objective statement.

I first became interested in Mary Anderson as a person in the early days of the Women's Bureau in the United States

Department of Labor. At that time it was one of my duties as a member of the staff of the bureau to assemble for interested authors material that could be used for magazine articles about the bureau and its personnel. Some enterprising journalist had submitted to us a very detailed questionnaire about Mary Anderson to be used in a short biographical sketch. Among many other things she was asked to describe the most interesting and important thing she had ever done. She had just returned from Paris where she had gone to confer with the members of the American delegation who were attending the Peace Conference after World War I. She had reported directly to President Wilson in Paris and had made many contacts with European women. This was her first return to Europe after she had left Sweden as an emigrant thirty-one years before. I was full of enthusiasm over the drama and significance of her trip and it seemed to me hardly necessary to ask this question. I thought I already knew the answer. But I was wrong. For when we came to it she hesitated for a moment and then replied that the most important and interesting thing she had ever done was her work on the Hart, Schaffner, and Marx agreement which established arbitration as a method of settling labor disputes.

This answer seemed to me then, and after many years of association with her it still seems, to give the clearest indication of one of the outstanding qualities which enabled her to rise to the eminent position she attained. She had worked on the Hart, Schaffner, and Marx agreement for two years at the very beginning of her working life as a trade unionist. Her contribution to the enforcement of that agreement was a comparatively minor one. She had been part of a team which reached its goal. It was indeed a most important event in the history of trade union negotiation, but so far as Mary Anderson herself was concerned it was the achievement and not her personal contribution that was important and interesting. She has never dramatized herself or her part in important issues of her time. Instead her interest has been entirely in the job to be done and in the results obtained.

Her story shows how she progressed from one task to another, accepting the responsibility that each entailed, gradually enlarging the scope and importance of her activities, without personal ambition, but with a complete dedication to the cause in hand. Time and again there are instances of her sturdy independence and enterprise, from the morning on the ship leaving Sweden when she was the member of the party who aroused herself from sea sickness to prepare coffee and food for the relief of her fellow sufferers, to the decision she made to confer with the delegates to the International Labor Organization in Geneva in spite of the fact that she had been directed by the secretary of labor not to attend the meetings.

Her life covers the whole range of experience of a working woman employed in the United States during a period of enormous changes in the status of women in the industrial, political, and social life of the country. Exploitation, bad working conditions, low wages, discriminations, were all part of her experience. So too were trade unionism, cooperation, education, and friendship. The account of how she profited by them all is an absorbing illustration of the possibilities inherent in the American community, and of the development of a personality through experience.

Her philosophy toward the problems of her time was based on the necessities she herself discovered. She joined the union because she was lonely and wanted friends, not because she had an exalted idea of what a union could do. She found that out later and learned her trade unionism by practical experience. She became an American citizen because she wanted to vote. She upheld the civil service system and the integrity of her work from political pressures, not because of an abstract theory about government, but because she knew that only so could she effectively administer a government bureau.

It has not been an easy task to extract from her the personal account which brings her to life for the reader. As she herself said when I asked her to describe her conversation with her brothers when she saw them again after thirty-five years, "Swedes don't talk much." Her story must unfold to the reader more by implication than by direct statement, but when it is unfolded, it gives a picture of a simple, strong, unemotional woman, of great integrity, who has had an extraordinary life and has made a great contribution to the advancement of women everywhere.

Mary N. Winslow

Table of Contents

*Illustrations between pages 52 and 53
and between pages 84 and 85*

Woman at Work

From the Old World to the New

THE United States has been my country for more than fifty years. I came here when I was sixteen years old. I could not speak English, I knew nothing of America, but I thought it was a land of opportunity and that was what I wanted. I have had a wonderful life in America. It has given me everything—friends, work, and a chance to do something in the world. Now that I have "retired" after twenty-five years as a worker in the service of the United States, it seems a good time to look back and make a record of some of the things that have happened to me, and of some of the developments that have come during the years I have worked in the labor movement, in the Women's Trade Union League, and in the Women's Bureau of the United States Department of Labor. I have had a lot of luck and a lot of fun, but I have worked hard, too, and I think I have helped get some things done that needed to be done. Anyway, I have done what I could and my memories of other days may add something useful to the record.

In America, my life has been spent almost entirely in cities, Chicago and Washington chiefly, but I started out on a farm in Sweden.

We were a big family, my father, my mother, and seven

3

children. I was the youngest. First there was my sister Anna, then came two brothers, Nicholas and Wilhelm, and a sister, Louise, then Hilda, Oscar, and I. Oscar was six years older and my oldest sister was twenty years older than I. My mother was small, not fat, but slender, with great big eyes and brown hair. I always thought she was very pretty. My father was tall, slender, and dark. His name was Magnus Anderson. Mother was born on her family's farm where Father was the overseer when they were married. After they were married they bought their own farm in the same neighborhood.

Mother was one of ten children and I had more cousins than I could count, living quite near by. My father's family was not big. He had a brother and sister who lived some way off so we did not see them much, but my mother's family often visited us. When they came they stayed for perhaps a week. We were very crowded, but this was good, particularly in winter, because it was hard to keep the house heated and the more people there were, the warmer it was. There was a great big wood-burning stove in each room, but I think we were often cold.

Our farm was about a mile from the little village of Lidköping in a very lovely part of Sweden, not far from Göteborg. In Sweden, the little farm villages are very much like those in Russia, small settlements of sometimes only ten houses, or even less. The buildings are more or less together and the farms are outside. This makes for a rather social life and the people are not isolated as they are on the farms in the United States. The country is rolling and hilly, with very pretty little mountains and lakes. It is very much like the country in Minnesota.

Our house was a five-room white wooden house with a red tile roof, as was usual there. Then there was a little house with two rooms for the men we hired to work on the farm. We had a very nice flower garden and also a vegetable garden. My mother liked the garden, but it was Father who was particularly interested in it, and we were noted for our flowers. I remember one peony bush that was especially lovely. When I went back to visit our house after I had been in the United States for more than thirty years, this bush was still there and the flowers were as lovely as ever. The blooming season is short, but since they have light night and day, as in the Arctic, the flowers grow quickly and their fragrance is wonderful.

Back of the house there was a small pond with a little bridge across it leading to the barn. In winter we used to drive a big stick into the middle of the pond, tie our sleds to it, and so have a little merry-go-round.

Our school was at the Lutheran parsonage, with one school-master and several teachers. The schoolmaster, who was an important person, was red-headed and had a terrible temper. I studied under him most of the time.

One year I sat next to a girl who was very comical. She said funny things to me all during school hours and I think all I did that term was laugh. The result was that I did not learn anything and did not pass my examination. This made me so ashamed that when I went back the next term I made up my mind I would study; I passed into the higher grade and when we graduated I was the first one in my class. If any question was asked in the class my hand always went up, but the schoolmaster would ignore me and ask others. Then, if they were not right, he would ask me.

We had examinations on the last day of school, Graduation Day. Our families came and sat around the sides of the room, while we were in our places in the center. The room was crowded with twenty-five to thirty children and their families. The families were especially interested because the Lutheran religion was also taught. We had examinations in every subject and it was a great ordeal. The master asked questions of each child about geography, spelling, and the other subjects we had studied. I was not very good in spelling, I never have been, but I was good in other subjects.

I had a good time as a child, in the family, at school, and

with other children, but I was very shy. If company came to
the house, unless I was in the room when they came, my
mother would have to drag me in to see them. I remember
always sitting on my mother's lap, even when I was a big
girl, and the other children would say, "Look at the big girl
sitting on Mother's lap." We had a dog who was very jealous
and once he jumped up and bit my hand when she had her
arms around me.

There was plenty of work to do and plenty of fun too. I
particularly loved the horses. We had about six. I used to get
them in from the pasture, riding bareback and racing with my
brothers. There was only one other girl to play with, so
my playtime was mostly spent with the boys and I never
played with dolls. We tobogganed on a deep ravine, down
which we went so fast that we kept on going up the far side.
We skied and had other winter sports on the pond. Sometimes we skated over the ice when it was very thin and one
evening when I was nine or ten years old I fell through, but
I held on to the edge of the ice and my brothers got me out.

I helped with chores, but I never liked to do work in the
house. We made everything we used — spinning, tanning
leather, and doing the slaughtering, curing, and salting. We
had a tailor who came to the house to make suits for the men,
a dressmaker for our dresses, and a shoemaker for the shoes.
They came at regular times in the fall and spring. If they
lived far away, they stayed with us until the things were finished.

We wore heavy underwear in the winter and several petti-
coats, one quilted, and then a dress. And we had what we
used a good deal over there, a coat with a fur lining, which
is much warmer than when the fur is on the outside. We wore
woolen scarfs on our heads, no hats. We wore scarfs in summer too. If we dressed up we had to have a white scarf, with
a fringe, like the ones worn in America now. My father used
to give us very lovely ones for Christmas. He bought them

in the town where he also went to market and to sell our eggs, butter, and milk, and sometimes meat, in the fall.

I hated to see the loom come into the room. I never liked that kind of work and never did any spinning. But I did knit some stockings. My sisters were very proficient weavers, making all sorts of patterns, mostly of wool, but some linen too. We raised our own flax. My mother was a very busy person, but I did not like anything in the way of housework. I did wash dishes, because I had to, but then I would get the boys to come in and ask if I could go out, so that I would escape the weaving and the other household chores.

We had to do our own thrashing, sometimes during the winter, because we did not have enough help to get it done at harvest time even though we had our own thrashing machine. I used to drive the horses around and around for the thrashing. It was terribly cold, but I loved the horses so much that I did not mind the cold.

There were terrific snows in winter with drifts three to four feet high. We had a well and we had to dig a passage to it and to the barns. Often the snow was so high that one could not see a person standing in the passage. The snows began before Christmas and lasted for many months.

The people in the village had to keep the roads open, and each year a foreman was appointed to see that they got out to shovel snow. One year when my father was foreman there was a dreadfully heavy snow and the men had to be notified to get to work. Some one of us had to tell them, so I rode one of the horses, bareback, to take the message. It must have been twenty to thirty degrees below zero and the crust was so hard the horse ran on top of it. That was no hardship for me.

The farming season was very short. In August it began to get dark early. In November and December, it was practically dark all day long. The light was from ten o'clock till about two o'clock. But there was no sun. In January, it was very cold, then the sun began to shine a little, and by March, although it was still cold, the sun was really bright. In June the sun shone almost all night and it was very beautiful.

In the summertime we stayed up very late, but in winter we went to bed very early because it was so dark and cold and dreary with the snow covering half of the windows sometimes.

In the winter we got our only light from the kerosene lamps and the candles we made ourselves. We had a couple of dozen sheep and it was during the slaughtering time that we made candles. We worked in the kitchen. I can see now the long sticks with three or four wicks on each stick. We dipped them into the tallow and then hung them on a rack. There would be as many as fifteen or twenty-five sticks. When we had finished with the last one it was time to begin again on the first one. There was a fire under the tallow all the time. It would take about a day to get the right size on a batch of candles. They were not as large as ours in the United States because the smaller ones burned better and did not drip.

I understand that now about ninety per cent of the farms in Sweden are lighted by electricity. In the farther parts of Sweden, near and inside the Arctic Circle, where the nights are very long for six months or more, they have electricity in the cities and towns, and in the mines, the lumber camps, and other such places, and the morale of the people is tremendously improved. They now have movies and dance halls, something to do during the darkness. I understand that electricity is very cheap and is furnished nearly everywhere so that the poorest kind of home can have light. I wish we had had that light when I was a child.

This was my life in Sweden as I remember it. Then misfortune overtook us.

On our farm the crops were always poor because there was quite a bit of low land and when there was much rain it became a marsh. I remember once when we had planted rye we did not have enough to sow again the next spring and what little we had was so poor we could not make dough properly. It would not get stiff enough. That situation existed for two years.

Our little farm belonged to the Crown, so my father and some of the other men went to Stockholm to ask the king about lowering the taxes. They got an audience with the king, but he said he could not lower the taxes, which amounted to rent for the farm and were very high, and so eventually we lost the farm.

My mother and father could not support us any longer and we knew that we had to get out and do something to earn a living, but we could not think what to do because there was no opportunity for anything except housework in our neighborhood. The solution came when my sister Anna, who had gone to America the year before, sent for Hilda and me to join her.

Anna was the first of the family to go to America. She was more than thirty years old when she decided to go. It was a time of tremendous emigration from Sweden, 1887, and she and a friend went over together. Mother and Father had recognized that it was the best thing for her to do, but it was hard to scrape up the money for her trip. She was outfitted by buying some nice dresses and a coat in town and arranging to pay for them later from America. Father made a fuss about that, but it was the only thing she could do.

She knew no English, but after she had settled in Pentwater, Michigan, she got a job as house worker for a family. Then she wrote and asked Hilda and me to come. Hilda was little and somewhat hard of hearing. She looked like my mother, but was rather frail. She and I had only worked at home before this and Father demurred about our leaving, but Mother said we had no chance in Sweden and she thought he should let us go. I think Mother was really a feminist and believed in women doing things they wanted to do, if they could. Father believed in being the head of the family, but he was very good-natured and was always doing good for others.

When we had finally made the decision it was very exciting getting ready to go. Our tickets by steerage cost about thirty dollars for each of us. We bought no special clothes, but went with the things we had.

I remember the parting in the early spring of 1889. I was only sixteen, very young and enthusiastic. The day before we were to leave I went to say good-by to a cousin who lived near us. While I was with her I became hysterical and could not stop crying, so when I went back home she went with me and stayed all night. We left about four o'clock in the morning. Father drove us to the station where we took the train. I had never been on a train before. We went to Göteborg, where we were to take the ship, and stayed all night with friends.

For the trip we were to join a family we knew, Mrs. Beck and three children, whose father was already in America. We took an old mattress because none were furnished on the boat. The Becks took cooking utensils and we took food — herring, sausage, hard bread, and coffee.

We had not been on board long before we ran into a storm and were terribly sick. There was no air in the large, dormitory-like place where we slept on bunks with blankets and a pillow on each but no mattresses except the ones we had brought with us. Men and women were all together with no privacy at all. There were a good many Finns on board. We couldn't understand them and did not like them anyway.

We were sick for hours. The captain came down to see us and I remember he held my hand for a time. Finally, I got a little better and went up on deck. After a while the Becks were better, too, but my sister was still sick. I took the coffeepot and the coffee and went to the kitchen to fix something hot to drink. When it was ready I took it down and we all had a little meal of bread and herring and coffee. After that we were all right.

In the evening there was a lull in the storm and we went on deck and danced and had a good time. The next evening we landed at Hull and stayed there nearly a week, living in a dormitory for women. Finally, we took the train to Liverpool, where we waited until the steamship *City of Paris* came along and we got on her. I had a little money my father had given me so I bought a hat in Liverpool. I had never had a hat before. As I remember, it was made of straw with some flowers on it. It was springtime, May 1889.

The *City of Paris* was a very good boat. We still traveled steerage, but the bunks had mattresses and food was served to the steerage passengers. We spent most of our time on deck. I was not seasick on that boat, although we had a terrible storm. I remember water coming down the steps to the cabin where we were. There were many Irish on board, whom we did not like any better than we had the Finns because they were very noisy.

After about ten days we got to New York where we stayed overnight. That evening there was a band concert in Battery Park and Hilda and I went to it. I bought fried cakes and coffee for my first food in America. We were told before leaving home not to go out at night with anyone, and we could not find our way around alone, so we slept that first night on the floor at Castle Garden.

When we first arrived we were examined through an interpreter, who asked us where we came from and what we were going to do. The only papers we had were certificates we had got from our pastor before leaving Sweden, but these papers and the information we gave through the interpreter seemed to be satisfactory and the next day, after some more examinations, guards furnished by the steamship company took us on a ferry to Hoboken to get the train.

We left in the afternoon for Grand Rapids, Michigan, where we arrived eventually about three in the morning. Here we had to change to another train that was there waiting. We got to Muskegon, Michigan, about five hours later

and had to change trains again. There, we were left in the
waiting room alone and we sat for hours waiting for our train
to come. We were tired and hungry and felt very forlorn.

While we were sitting there, with our bags and bundles
surrounding us and the Beck children fretful and tired, about
eleven in the morning a Danish man came along and said that
he lived on top of the hill above the station and he wanted
us all to come up to his house where his wife would give us
food and let us rest. We were very chary of accepting his
invitation, but finally after great coaxing, we went with him
and had some good food, the first real meal we had had since
leaving the ship. We were so afraid of missing the train that
the minute we had eaten we went back to the station. There
we waited until eight thirty in the evening, not knowing when
a train would come by. When one came at last, I went out
and motioned that we wanted to get on. It was not until we
were settled on this train that we discovered we were just one
hour from Pentwater.

When we got there everyone was at the train to meet us,
my sister and all her friends. We had a wonderful welcome
and then we went to bed and slept until the next afternoon.
We stayed in Pentwater only a short time as Anna was going
to Ludington, Michigan, for a job.

2

A Casual Worker in the Promised Land

WHEN I left Sweden I had the idea that America was a promised land because I felt that there might be something other than household work that a person like me could do. I had heard about what other people, emigrants, were doing. They had written back very glowingly. But when I got to America, I found that housework was almost the only job I could get.

Leaving Pentwater, after about two days, we took the boat to the lumbering town of Ludington, Michigan. Anna wanted to get away from Pentwater because it was so small there was not much opportunity for anyone. She got a place in Ludington and very shortly became acquainted with a widower and married. Then the problem was to get places for Hilda and me. Hilda found a job very quickly and also was soon married. So both of them were settled quickly.

I got a place in a lumberjack's boardinghouse washing dishes. It was very hard work. I think I got two dollars a week and my board and lodging. We had to carry water and look out for fifteen or twenty lumberjacks. It was early morning work — and all-day-long work. There were a cook and two other women for house cleaning, making beds, and laying the table, but I didn't know much of the language and I had nobody to talk to. It seemed to me that there was nothing in my life but dirty dishes to wash and a kitchen to clean up. I remember that my prospective brother-in-law brought me a present one day of some red, white, and blue ribbons, but I just kept them put away, because there was no place I could go to show them off and nothing else I could do with them.

After about a month I left the boardinghouse and went to work for a Norwegian girl who had married the son of the man who owned the sawmill. They had a lovely new house and one child about four years old. I did the laundry and had to wash and iron a lot of dresses for the child and I did not like it. After all, I was only sixteen years old and I was never a very good ironer. Besides the washing and ironing, I did all the housework and the cooking and waited on table. I was paid a dollar and a half a week.

I did not like the woman I worked for, she was very haughty. I was not sorry after four or five months when they moved away and I got a job with another family, a mother and son, where I worked for four or five months doing the cooking and housework for two dollars a week. The work there was not as hard as in the other place, but soon the son got married and the household broke up, so I was out of work again.

By that time I had learned a little English by listening to what people said and by reading the morning paper over and over again until finally it occurred to me what the words meant. I learned quite a bit that way and then when the words were spoken I understood them.

Then I got a job with a family named Dowlan. He was owner of the sawmill in Ludington and was also the mayor of the town. They had a family of grown children. One son was married, another was in college, a daughter had already finished college, a younger son, about seventeen or eighteen, was a sort of ne'er-do-well. Mrs. Dowlan was a lovely woman. She did not do any cooking so I had to do it all, but if we had anything nice she always came out and told me how good it was. She took me to church with her and taught me a great deal about English.

I worked there almost a year. I got three dollars a week, but I had very little time off. On Sundays I was free after dinner and Sunday evenings I went to my sisters' homes, where we saw a good many friends, mostly Swedes we had known at home. One Sunday I heard that Hilda's husband, Pete Larson, was going to Ashland, Wisconsin, to work in a lumber camp. He was moving his family there—they had a young child by that time—and they wanted me to go with them. He went ahead of us and sent for us in the fall. My sister Anna did not want me to go but I wanted to do something different, and so we went, Hilda, the baby, and I.

It was quite a trip from Ludington. Pete met us and took us out to our house on the edge of the camp in a sleigh. I never liked it very much there; it was not like Sweden. My sister did not like it either, but we stayed all winter.

After we had been there a few months Pete broke his leg and was taken to the hospital at Ashland. When he was brought home I used to look after his leg and fix his bandages. He told me how they had done it at the hospital and I have been able to do bandaging ever since.

We never went into the camp itself. Our house was built of logs and had two bedrooms; a big stove kept us warm. It was very comfortable but very lonesome. When I had time I studied English from some English readers, with Pete's help. Once in a while one or two of the men would come in and talk, but my brother-in-law didn't want them around much. They were mostly pretty hard characters. They would work about a month, draw their wages, and go off to town. Then, when their money was spent, they would come back for more work. There were no other women near the camp.

In the spring, my sister Anna wrote that she and her husband were moving to Chicago. Because of the World's Fair, there was going to be a great deal of building and he wanted to work there. She asked if I would go with them, and I decided to leave the camp.

After I left, Hilda and her husband moved into a little town across Lake Superior from Ashland where they lived until she died when she was forty-eight years old. She had a number of children, Albert, Mary, Pearl, Carl, and Bill.

I got back to Ludington one morning and we left that afternoon on a boat for Chicago. My brother-in-law, Frank Lind, found a place in West Pullman working on a World's Fair building. It was not far from Chicago and was a beautiful place on the lake with good working conditions.

We joined him there and then my life in the factory began. I suppose my experience for the next few years was like that of any other girl who goes from one job to another looking for security and decent wages and living conditions. In our neighborhood there was a shoe factory and a garment factory. I got my first job in the garment factory doing hand finishing on trousers. I did not like the work, and after a few weeks, I went to the shoe factory and got a job there. They put me on a "top stitcher" machine that stitched and cut the edges at the same time. I was paid three dollars a week while learning and I got very tired just "learning" and not really doing anything. After some weeks, I went down to the lining section and said I would like to work there. In the stitching section I had had a very nasty forewoman, who, when she found out what I had done, came over to the lining section and just "gave it to me" for leaving the work I had been assigned to. She said she had been trying to do the best thing for me and sent me back to her section. Then she put me on real work, not "learning" any more, and in three weeks I was doing piecework and making eight dollars a week. That was more than anyone else in the factory made and I was "cock of the walk" for a while.

I never got bored with that job because fitting the lining to the outside and stitching it had to be done carefully or else the next process, "vamping," could not be done. I always look back on my life in that factory, where six or seven hundred people worked, as very interesting because this was my first factory experience and I learned that factory life is not just the work at a machine. You make contacts with other people. You talk to the person at the machine on each side of you, sometimes about your work, sometimes about your people and your life at home, sometimes about parties and boy friends. If you like one another (and that is not always) you become very friendly because you spend ten or twelve hours a day together. In that factory at lunch time we used to gather together for a half-hour around one of the big stitching tables. One of the girls would make coffee or tea for which we paid ten cents a week. Then we would have our own sandwiches and plenty of conversation. Some of the girls were very amusing, especially the Irish. To me it was all great fun and was something I needed very badly because, after all, I was a greenhorn.

Our working conditions, lighting, and sanitation were pretty good for the times. We worked ten hours a day, from seven thirty in the morning until six in the afternoon, with a half-hour off for lunch. I was not a member of the union in those days. As I remember it, there was no union in our factory, but one day some people from Chicago came and wanted us to join. We were willing and the company was willing, but the union people never came back. I didn't know what a union was, but I was ready to join because I wanted to be with others and do what they were doing, and that is what I thought the union meant.

By that time I spoke English on the job. I spoke it fairly well because my sister and brother-in-law and I never talked Swedish, but instead used English all the time.

After about a year my sister and her husband moved back to Ludington. One of the women who worked as a button-hole maker in the factory joined me and we kept house together in the same house that my sister had left.

Finally, the firm we worked for failed, and somebody suggested that we go to Dixon, where Wells Fargo had a factory. We went and found it was a beautiful place. We lived in a very nice boardinghouse and worked ten hours a day.

One day we were told that the Illinois legislature had passed an eight-hour law and that we would work only eight hours a day. We thought it was wonderful, but we worked eight hours only one day and then we were told that the court had said the law was unconstitutional. This was my first experience with hour laws for women. I did not suspect at the time how much of my life was going to be spent trying to get such laws enacted and enforced. Nor did I know that Jane Addams and Mrs. Florence Kelley, who had been chiefly responsible for the enactment of that eight-hour law and the one day of enforcement, would become good friends of mine in a few years.

We stayed in Dixon about eight months and then work became slack, so we went back to Chicago. We could not find any jobs there, and when we heard that a firm in Milwaukee was looking for help we decided to try our luck with them. We stayed only a few months because we did not like the place. The pay was poor, eight or nine dollars a week, and the working conditions were bad — we were in an old building which was dirty, crowded, and unsanitary.

After that a firm in Neenah, Wisconsin, sent people to Milwaukee looking for help. We went there for about six months, but we did not like the work very well, and when things got slack we went back to Chicago. We had no money and had to take a cheap room on North Clark Street, which was not a very desirable neighborhood, but we had no difficulties while we were there.

By that time it was spring and we felt we had to have new hats. We had very little money, but that did not keep us from getting the hats. I paid four dollars for mine, a great big thing that turned up off the face. The next Sunday we took a walk in the park and people kept looking at us. We were very conscious of our new finery and thought the people were staring at us because the hats were terrible; we never wore them again after that afternoon.

Then I got a job at Schwab's in Chicago and my friend got a job making buttonholes in a shirtwaist factory. I made from twelve to fourteen dollars a week. It was a good job and I worked there for seven years.

3

The Young Trade Unionist

BY the time I got the job at Schwab's in Chicago I was twenty-two years old. I had been in America about six years and had had ten different jobs. During that time I had progressed from housework at a dollar and a half a week to a skilled job in the shoe industry at about fourteen dollars a week. I had learned English, had made a few friends, and had seen something of life in a number of different places. I was not a "greenhorn" any more, but I had not had time or money to learn much about what was going on outside my job.

The seven years I spent at Schwab's marked my entrance into the trade union movement. Although I did not know it at the time, this was to be the real beginning of life for me in America. For six years I had been a casual worker, going from one job to another, doing what I could to earn a living. I was independent. If I did not like a job, I quit and got another. But after I went to Schwab's and joined the union I found that it was not always necessary to change jobs to get better working conditions. Sometimes we could improve conditions through union negotiations with the employer. That was a better way, because then conditions were improved for a great many people and not just for the one person who changed to a better job.

I did not know anything about the union when I first joined. A business agent for the Boot and Shoe Workers Union came to the factory and asked some of the girls if they would join. The girls asked me. I wanted to go along with them just to be friendly but I said I would like to know something about it first. We all went to a meeting, heard that a union would mean better wages and shorter hours, and then we joined. After a few weeks I became the shop collector for the union and in about a year I was elected president of the Stitchers Local 94 of the International Boot and Shoe Workers Union. I was president of that local for about fifteen years. The members of most of the locals in the union were men. But in our stitchers local the members were all women. Schwab's was a union factory, and we had about one hundred and fifty stitchers in our local.

The union work took a great deal of my time in the evenings, but I was willing — more than willing — to give it. In addition to being president of the local I was also a delegate to the joint council of the union, composed of delegates from each local. It was this joint council that made the decisions about asking for wage increases or better working conditions. I was elected too by my local to be a delegate to the Chicago Federation of Labor, which held meetings every other Sunday afternoon. And finally, after some years, I was elected a member of the executive board of the International Boot and Shoe Workers Union.

It was late in 1894 when I first went to work at Schwab's. I spent all my spare time on trade union matters and did not have a chance to supplement my education at night school or by studying at home. We worked a ten-hour day, from seven thirty in the morning until six in the afternoon. I would have to start to work very early because it was a long walk from my home on the North Side of the city to the factory on the West Side. After work was over I would go home for supper and then I was usually off to meetings that sometimes lasted very late. Fortunately, I was strong and well and enjoyed the work I was doing, so it was not too hard on me physically.

During those seven years at Schwab's I learned a great deal about the work and discipline that is necessary for trade unionists. For instance, very often we had a lot of trouble with our machines. When the machines broke down we lost time, and because we were on piecework, lost time meant lost money. The firm usually did not have enough experienced machinists to fix the machines quickly, so we had to wait around and lose more time than was necessary. This was a matter we had to straighten out through our shop committees and sometimes it took a long while. We had to learn to be patient, which was not easy because we were not earning anything while we waited.

Sometimes there was difficulty between the workers. If a girl managed in some way to get hold of a batch of work that was easier than what she should have had, we all knew it and resented it. If she did this too often we would call it to the attention of the foreman and he would straighten it out.

There were many other such small matters that had to be attended to from day to day, but we got so that we could take them calmly and not make too much fuss. Thus I found by experience that it is the drudgery of doing little things and hammering away to get a little improvement here and a change for the better there that really counts for the most in the long run. I learned too that strikes are spectacular and exciting and sometimes dramatize a situation as nothing else can, but on the whole they involve so much suffering that I think every good trade unionist wants to avoid a strike if possible and only use it as a last resort. Often strikes are the only way out and are absolutely necessary, but sometimes they are not justified and in that case they do harm to the whole trade union movement.

One day we had a strike like that at Schwab's. The men went out and the women went out with them, although we had a contract with the firm not to strike but to arbitrate any grievances. The next day some of the men had calmed down and wanted to go back to work. The general office of the union, in Boston, had sent word we would get no strike benefit because we had broken our contract. But the women refused to go back and said to the men, "No, if you think you have a grievance bad enough to want to strike about, we will stay out until that grievance is settled." That evening the superintendent came and talked with us and said he would take up the grievance in the morning; we went back to work the next day and learned something about the value of arbitration and the foolishness of wildcat strikes.

The seven years I spent at Schwab's were a kind of apprenticeship for me in trade union work. Our union did not have much money and was not able to do much but it accomplished something. We on the joint council took up all kinds of grievances that came along in the different factories and tried to get shorter hours and better wages. One of our problems was the changes in style which brought changes in the stitching and other work we had to do. We were all on piecework and the employers wanted to set the rate of pay on the basis of the speediest workers while we wanted to set it on average production. Setting the rate in one factory did not mean that it would apply in others, so we had plenty of work to do, particularly since the styles were always changing.

Another problem was the amount of slack time, when the work did not come through and we had to sit around the factory for hours with nothing to do. Because we were on piecework it was our time that was wasted, not the company's time. Often we would come in at the regular hour in the morning and have to wait until nearly lunch time to get a bit of work. While we were waiting we used to beg the foreman to let us go home. The little work there was could accumulate so that we would have something worth while to do the next day. He seldom granted our request and that created a great deal of resentment. We also felt that he knew in advance when work would be slack and if he had had any consideration for us he would have told us the night before that it would be all right if we did not come until late the next day.

These kinds of grievances do not sound very important but they can mount up and result in a great deal of bad feeling with a consequent loss in output and earnings. It was an important part of the union's work to get such things settled quickly.

After I had worked at Schwab's for seven years they went out of business and I got a job with Selz and Company, a very big place with about one thousand workers, of whom about three hundred were women. I was the only person in the stitching room who belonged to the union, but I was still president of Local 94. After a while when the factory across the street went on strike, I used to take up collections for the strikers. Sometimes I would get twenty-five or thirty dollars in a collection, but I had to stop because my foreman said if they heard about it in the office it would not look very well for me. The strike was about over by then, anyway, and it did not seem worth while to make an issue of it.

After I had been at Selz's for about a year the Boot and Shoe Workers Union had some trouble with the workers in Lynn, Massachusetts. The workers in several firms there had struck in spite of their agreement to arbitrate all grievances. Our secretary-treasurer came to Chicago and wanted some of us who were responsible trade unionists to go to Lynn and help fulfill the terms of the agreement. Quite a few of us, about a dozen men and women, agreed to go and we set out together to get jobs in the shoe factories of Lynn. The union paid our traveling expenses and helped with our living expenses because the wages in Lynn were very low. I got a job for fourteen dollars a week doing very low-grade work, which was all the Lynn factories turned out at that time. As soon as we got into a factory and became acquainted with the workers, we would persuade them to come to a meeting, where we would reorganize them and impress on them their responsibility to carry out the union agreement with the employers.

We were able to do quite a bit while we were there. We got some of the workers reorganized and back to work and I became the president of the women's local in Lynn. When I left after about a year they gave me a very beautiful watch which I still have.

When I got back to Chicago I went to work again at Selz's. I had been back about two weeks when my troubles began. The vampers went on strike and the whole factory went out with them because of a grievance about wages. Except for a very few, the workers were not members of the union and they went out against my advice. I thought the grievance was very small and that if they made a real effort it could be settled without a strike. But they went out just the same and the foreman thought, because I was a member of the union, that I had instructed them to go out. So I was condemned by both the workers and the firm, and lost my job.

I was out of work for about two months. It was a terrible time. I lived with my sister, who had moved back to Chicago, but I had absolutely no money. Work was slack everywhere and I could not get a job. I tried everywhere I knew of, but it seemed as if there were no jobs; I just could not go back to Selz's and ask to be taken on again. I learned then what a heartbreaking experience it is to have no job and to look hopelessly for work. That is the nightmare of all wage earners, and too often it becomes a reality and not just apprehension.

Finally, one of my friends spoke to the foreman in the Smith Shoe Company and I worked there until the foreman of Selz's sent for me, said that he had found out I had not been the one to instigate the strike, and told me to come in and bring my lunch and go to work, which I did.

I worked there for about a year until one day the foreman came to me and said, "You're fired." I did not know why. I was so stunned I could not even ask why I was fired. As I went out I met one of my friends who was coming in for half a day's work. She asked me why I was leaving and when she found out I did not know the cause of my trouble she asked the foreman, who said I had spoiled a whole case of shoes, about twelve pairs. I was sure I had not, but there was nothing I could do about it. The union was not strong enough at Selz's to intercede for me.

I got work then in a little factory where I stayed for some time. Eventually the foreman at Selz's sent for me and said he had found out that it was not my fault the shoes were spoiled; the linings had been cut wrong. He asked me to come back, but I was so hurt I could not. Instead, I stayed on in the little factory and it was there I had my first practical experience with the effects on production of overtime work. In later years I was to spend much effort on demonstrating the fact that greater production does not always result from longer hours. I learned this from my own experience.

In this factory the foreman used to try to increase production by working the employees overtime. About five or five thirty in the afternoon he would say, "We are going to work till nine tonight." We had no food and our families did not know where we were. When we finally got home we were so tired and mad that the next morning we stayed out "sick." One week we worked three nights. After the second night about one third and after the third night about one half of the factory stayed out. When he counted up the production for that week the foreman said we had produced less than when we worked the regular full-time hours in the daytime. We never worked at night again. This experience helped me considerably in later years, especially when we were trying to limit night work for women in the war industries in 1917 and in 1941.

After I had worked in this little place for a few months I went back to Smith's for five years. At that time organizing women was very difficult. The unions were unpopular because the girls were afraid they would lose their jobs if they joined, and their general attitude toward unions was that only roughnecks belonged to them. Two other girls and I were the only union members at Smith's, but whenever there was any trouble we had to settle it.

There were two sisters in the plant whom we used to call the "Shetland ponies" because they were so full of energy and bounce. One of them was named Kit and both were great favorites. One day Kit's sister came dashing through the plant calling, "Stand up, girls! Stand up! Kit's fired!" We all stood up, which meant that the work stopped. The foreman came along and asked why we were standing up so I proceeded to tell him. He said, "Do you know why she's fired?" I answered, "I understand it is for bad work, but we do not believe it." Without a word he walked over and picked up some of the work Kit had done and showed it to me. I took one look and went back to my machine. It *was* poor work. We never stood up after that and never did anything else unless we were sure of our facts. It was a good lesson and I am glad I learned it because it was always helpful to me afterward.

We had a lot of fun at Smith's. Sometimes the machines broke down and we could not work. Then we danced, told jokes, laughed, and made considerable noise. One day when the power was off our foreman was on one of the lower floors and another foreman said, "You'd better go up on your floor. There's a terrible noise up there." Our foreman said, "You mind your own business," and he wouldn't go up until the power started again. Then he told us about it and said, "But, for heaven's sake, don't do it again. It *was* a terrible noise!"

In those years from 1905 to 1910 while I was at Smith's I got a great deal more experience in the labor movement and I began making contacts with others interested in the problems of labor through Hull House and Jane Addams, and finally through Mrs. Raymond Robins and the Women's Trade Union League.

Also, although I always had difficulty in getting away because the factory did not want me to leave, I went to Boston twice a year to attend meetings of the executive board of the International Boot and Shoe Workers Union. On numerous occasions the foreman said to me, "If you want that job, and have to go for the union, have the union put you on their payroll and keep you there." I knew there was no chance of the union's doing that, in spite of the fact that I was the only one of the board not on the union payroll. I was the only woman on the board and I wanted to stay on it, so I persuaded the foreman to let me off. I felt that my position on the board was an important one. I had been elected by the members of the national union to succeed Emma Steghagen, who had been the first woman on the board and was a fellow worker and great friend of mine. She left the board to become secretary of the Chicago Women's Trade Union League and then it was up to me to keep a toehold for women in this great union. The work of the board was to set the policies on which the individual contracts that would be negotiated in the various localities should be based. We also had to administer the sick and death benefits to which union members were entitled, and we were responsible for strike benefits and therefore had to authorize the calling of strikes. It was a responsible position and gave me a wide knowledge of conditions throughout the industry.

My life outside the factory was devoted almost entirely to meetings—not only our own regular meetings in the Boot and Shoe Workers Union, but also those of the Chicago Federation of Labor to which I was a delegate. Then there were special meetings. Except for the Chicago federation, which met on alternate Sunday afternoons, all meetings were in the evening.

It was through the discussions at these meetings that I began to get an over-all picture of the conditions under which the workers were employed in many different industries. The business of each meeting generally was to talk over complaints that were brought forward by individual workers or their spokesmen. We would hear their stories, then general discussion would follow, and we would decide what should be done. Many meetings, especially those of the Boot and Shoe

Workers Union, were devoted entirely to setting wage standards for the different operations in the industry and to outlining wage policies that would be discussed later with the employers. Because nearly all the operations in a shoe factory are piecework, whenever there was a change of style or operation, new piece rates had to be set. This was a job that took up the time of many meetings. But the meetings also served as general forums for airing the problems of the workers and presented an opportunity for those with grievances to blow off steam, which was sometimes very useful!

While I was a delegate to the Chicago Federation of Labor, I had my first experience with the bitter battles that sometimes took place among the different elements inside the trade union movement. I remember well one Sunday when we had an election of officers for the Chicago Federation of Labor. Most of us had cast our ballots for John Fitzpatrick, who we felt would give stability to the federation. Fitzpatrick had started his working life as a horse-shoer and even in the early days he displayed all the qualities which eventually made him a leading factor in the trade union movement. He was a big, broad-shouldered, manly looking fellow with lovely blue eyes and bushy black eyebrows. If he had any respect for you in any way you could always depend on him to be your friend. But in spite of the overwhelming support for him, there was one group of delegates, led by Martin B. (Skinny) Madden, who were against him. When the voting was over this group pounced upon the ballot boxes and got away with them. They then announced that Fitzpatrick had been defeated and Madden elected. But since the federation officials had not been able to count the ballots, they declared the election unconstitutional.

Shortly after this I was approached by the Madden crowd one evening after I had attended a meeting downtown. They told me that they would elect me to any position I wanted in the federation if I would go on their ticket. I ran out of the hall, jumped on a streetcar just as it was starting, and got

away from them that way. Later I reported the incident to
the officers of the federation.

For the next meeting we moved from Bricklayers' Hall on
the West Side, where it was easy for the opposition to get a
rough crowd to do what was wanted, to the North Side and
had another election. This time we had police protection and
everything went all right.

We then had a meeting in Bricklayers' Hall to announce
the election. After Emma Steghagen and I were seated, one
of the teamsters came back to us, the only women present, and
asked us to leave the hall right away because he knew there
would be shooting. We said we could stand it if they could,
and refused to leave.

The secretary of the federation, Edward N. Nockles, had
taken the ballot boxes, sealed them tightly, and put them in a
wall safe. The hall was packed, particularly in the back, and
in the front seats were a whole row of police. The meeting
was opened and went along well until the announcement of
the election and then the people in the back began to surge
forward and to shout, "Get Nockles." The policemen jumped
on the stage and arrested the presiding officers instead of stop-
ping the mob, but Nockles jumped off the stage and was
across the street before they ever got to him.

In the crowd that had surged up from the back of the hall
we recognized characters from the underworld of Chicago,
and the meeting was quickly adjourned. Two weeks later,
when we met again, Fitzpatrick had been declared president
in an executive board meeting, after the tally had been reported to the executive committee. Everything went smoothly
after that and it was certainly a fine thing for the federation
when they got Fitzpatrick as president.

One of the big organizations that belonged to the Chicago
Federation of Labor was the Chicago Teachers Federation led
by Margaret Haley. The teachers at that time were trying
to get a revaluation for tax purposes of certain property in
the city, particularly that of the *Chicago Tribune*. Their idea

was that the increased taxes resulting from this revaluation should be applied to increases in teachers' salaries. This required state legislation, and though the teachers had the full support of the Chicago Federation of Labor, it took years and much agitation to get this legislation passed. And then, unfortunately, the teachers did not get the increase. It was given instead to the Chicago policemen and it took years more of agitation and work on the part of the teachers before they got any increase.

During the fifteen years that I was a member of the Chicago Federation of Labor we participated in almost every effort for federal and state legislation to improve conditions for the workers. We also often had to put forth all our effort just to defeat legislation that would have been detrimental. In addition we cooperated with our constituent unions in supporting strikes and assisting negotiations wherever possible.

4

Women's Trade Union League

AFTER I joined the union I began to know Jane Addams and Hull House. We had meetings at Hull House, where Miss Addams would speak to us, and sometimes I would meet her at trade union meetings and in other places. It was always interesting to go to Hull House. Sometimes Miss Addams would ask us to come for tea on Sunday afternoons and we would meet prominent people from other parts of the country and from abroad. Among many others I remember especially meeting Keir Hardie and Ramsay MacDonald. I can see Miss Addams now, as she turned from person to person at these informal meetings, with her wonderful tact and understanding, her deep-set eyes soft and shining with interest, making everyone feel at home and bringing out the best in all of us. It was a splendid opportunity for us, who knew so little outside of our own work, to find out what other people were doing and thinking. We began to feel that we were part of something that was more important than just our own problems. For me, and I think for many others too, Hull House and Jane Addams opened a door to a larger life.

When I got back from Lynn and was working again in Chicago, I made my first contact with the Women's Trade Union League. I had been in Boston attending the conferences of the American Federation of Labor at the time the league

was organized there in 1903, but I did not have any part in it
at the beginning.

Emma Steghagen first told me about the league and asked
me to join it. Emma had been a fellow worker in Schwab's
factory. Her machine had been in front of mine. She was
older than I and was already in the trade union movement,
acting as secretary of her local. When it came to any trade
union activities she was the first person I turned to. In the
Women's Trade Union League she was always called "Sister
Emma" and that is what she seemed like to me. At that time
Jane Addams was president of the Chicago league. I was glad
to join because I knew that an organization of this sort would
be a great help to all working women.

The league was founded as a result of the suggestions of a
few trade unionists and people interested in the organization
of women. They thought it would help the organization of
women and would give an opportunity to people who were
sympathetic to unions, but were not actually workers, to join
as "allies" and work together with the trade unionists. The
first constitution of the league stated that membership was
open to "any person — who will declare himself or herself
willing to assist those trade unions already existing, which
have women members, and to aid in the formation of new
unions of women wage workers." The membership consisted
of individual working women, some of whom were trade
union members, men and women "allies," and a number of
affiliated unions.

There was a great field of work for the league in Chicago
(and everywhere else too). Working conditions for women
workers were very poor, as I knew from my own experience,
and very few women were organized. In fact, the men did
not seem anxious to get women organized because they had
all they could do to attend to their own grievances. Trade
union organization at that time was in the pioneer stage.
Except for the building trades, organization was very spotty,
there were active locals only here and there, and the men

said, "Let us organize the men first and then the women."
When it was organized, therefore, the league had a unique
position. It could take into its membership both men and
women workers and others who were not actually factory
workers but were sympathetic to the purpose of the league.
The members of the league united because they understood
that the union was at that time the only agency through
which the workers could defend their rights and that women
workers had to take their places along with the men. The
trade union men accepted that idea reluctantly, but they used
the league whenever they found they could be helped by it.

From its earliest days the league always tried to help the
unions and thus established a relationship that it was to carry
on in the future. When there were strikes and the strikers
could not get a place to meet they were always allowed to
use Hull House and were encouraged in every way. When
there was picketing and picketers were arrested, Miss Addams
would go to the employers and plead for them.

Miss Addams was the first president of the Chicago league.
She was followed by Mary McDowell who was president
until 1907. Miss McDowell was head of the University Settlement and had been a leader in the organization of the
women in the stockyards in 1902 and 1903 before the Wom-
en's Trade Union League was founded. She lived in the stockyards district and was close to the workers as a friend and
support. She was a heroic figure, tall and beautiful to look at,
with a vigorous, amusing, and friendly personality. The
stockyards workers had such admiration for her that they
called her the "Angel of the Stockyards." She was very fond
of parties and whenever we girls who were her friends
wanted a party we used to celebrate Mary McDowell's birth-
day — sometimes three or four times a year. It was around
Miss McDowell and Miss Addams, in the early days, that the
whole movement for the organization of women and the improvement of their working conditions centered.

As soon as I joined the league I began to spend more and

more of my free time at its meetings and parties. I will never forget my first speech shortly after I joined the league. The General Federation of Women's Clubs had a meeting at Hull House and Agnes Nestor, a glove worker, Josephine Casey, a ticket seller on the elevated railways, and I were scheduled to make speeches. I had never made one before and while waiting to be called on I must have looked ghastly. My knees shook so I was afraid I could not stand up. Josephine took a look at me and said, "Are you nervous?" I replied that I was just about dying but she said not to worry because the audience would not understand what I was saying anyway.

I spoke for about five minutes on hazards in industry and the lack of guards on machinery. I made the headlines in the papers because it was a very touchy subject and one that was to the fore at the time.

I knew of the hazards from experience in my own work as well as from what I was told by others. In our shop, the belting came up from the floor without much guarding and some belts came from overhead with no guards at all. The button machine and the eyelet machine were both dangerous too. Fingers were often caught in them. Besides, I had heard about dangers in other industries at the meetings of the Trade Union League.

It was at these meetings that I began to make the friendships that have lasted throughout the years. I will never forget them and the work and fun we had together. Among my earliest friends were Emma Steghagen and Agnes Johnson. They were both shoe workers. Then there was Agnes Nestor. She was a short, frail girl with great organizing and administrative ability; she was also a fine speaker. I got to know her soon after I joined the league. She was a glove worker and the glove workers and shoe workers were among the stanchest friends of the league throughout the years. Agnes was eventually elected president of the Chicago league after Mrs. Robins (who had succeeded Miss McDowell in 1907) resigned in 1913, and she was a lifelong leader in working for legislation for women workers in Illinois.

Elisabeth Christman was another of the glove workers with whom I started a lifelong friendship through the league. The glove workers and the shoe workers always used to say that they were cousins because one took care of the hands and the other of the feet. Elisabeth eventually became secretary-treasurer of the Chicago league and then secretary-treasurer of the national league, until it was dissolved in 1950. She was also for many years secretary-treasurer of the International Glove Workers Union. Only one other woman in the trade union movement (Sarah Conboy of the United Textile Workers) has held such a position.

Elisabeth was a lovely looking girl, with masses of beautiful brown hair. She always had great enthusiasm for anything she did and could work at high speed and very efficiently. She had such a friendly, lively nature that she was popular everywhere and her friends always respected her for her honest convictions and the way she worked for the cause of women and the trade union movement. She first went to Washington during the early days of World War I, about the same time I did. Later when the national league moved its headquarters, she settled in Washington permanently and our close association has continued through the years.

Other close friends of those days were Elizabeth Maloney of the waitresses' union, Mary McEnerny, business agent for the bindery workers, and later on Agnes Burns, who was a miner's daughter and was very active in the work of the league.

Then there were in the office of the league Stella Franklin and Alice Henry, two Australians who were not trade union women but were "allies" in the league. They did much to shape the policies of the league in the early days and were largely responsible for getting out *Life and Labor*, the monthly magazine published by the league for many years.

I made many good friends of other "allies" in the league

too. Among them, Mrs. Samuel Dauchy and her sister-in-law Beatrix Dauchy were to become lifelong friends, with whom I have never lost touch. All these friends and countless others filled my life with energy and enthusiasm. In fact, they and the things we were doing together were my life much more than the hours I spent at the factory. The factory work now was only a way to make money so that I could live and do my part in these other things.

There was one friend who stood out above all — Mrs. Raymond Robins. From the time I first knew her until the day of her death in 1945, she was our inspiration and support. I remember well when she first came to Chicago, the bride of Raymond Robins. Mr. Robins had lived in Chicago for some time and was a friend of Miss Addams and Mary McDowell. When he married Margaret Dreier, who was president of the New York Women's Trade Union League, he brought her to Chicago after their honeymoon and we had a meeting at Hull House to greet her. She was a most beautiful woman, tall, slender, dark, with wonderful eyes. She became a member of the Chicago league immediately and from that time on she was the mainspring of our work. Almost everything we undertook to do was at her inspiration. She was always seeing far ahead what could be done. Sometimes we were aghast at what she thought we could do, but finally it was unfolded before our eyes and it was done.

The Robinses lived in a tenement in the Seventeenth Ward, on the northwest side of the city. The Seventeenth Ward, in those days, was called the Bloody Seventeenth because on election days there were always riots and bloodshed there. Mr. Robins chose that place to live in because he did political and social work in the district. Their apartment was on the top floor, four flights up, and most of the other people who lived in the tenement were Italian garment workers. We used to go there to talk things over with Mrs. Robins, who was always understanding and helpful. After a short time, in 1907, we elected her president of the Chicago league, because Miss

McDowell, who was the president then, was so busy and lived so far away that she wanted to turn over the presidency to Mrs. Robins, who had more time.

At the first national convention of the league in 1907, Mrs. Robins was elected national president and from that time until 1922 when she resigned the presidency, she was our leader in the work of the league. I think I can sum up best what she meant to us all by saying that she gave us our chance. She never failed to help when help was needed and to encourage us when we were tired and depressed. She was the finest person I ever knew, and my gratitude to her will never end.

In the autumn of 1910 when I was still working at Smith's and spending my free time mostly on Women's Trade Union League activities, the great strike of the Chicago garment workers began. The strike started with a handful of girls walking out from one of the shops in the Hart, Schaffner, and Marx factory, the biggest clothing factory in town. Very soon the workers in the clothing industry all over town were out, until within a few weeks more than forty thousand were on strike. They were not organized, they just walked out because of accumulated grievances through the years.

Conditions in the industry were really bad. Piece rates were so low that the workers earned at best only a starvation wage and even this wage was often reduced by a system of unjust fines, as in one plant where any worker who damaged a pair of pants was made to buy them at the regular wholesale price. The story of one group of workers that was reported to the league illustrates the plight of most of them:

"We started to work at seven thirty and worked until six with three quarters of an hour for lunch. Our wages were seven cents for a pair of pants, or one dollar for fourteen pairs. For that we made four pockets and one watch pocket, but they were always changing the style of the stitching and until we got the swing of the new style, we would lose time and money and we felt sore about it. One day the foreman told us the wages were cut to six cents a pair of pants and the new style had two watch pockets. We would not stand for that, so we got up and left."

After they had been out for a very short time the workers turned to the United Garment Workers Union for help. This union found that the strike was so large that they could not cope with it alone, and they turned to the Chicago Federation of Labor and to the Women's Trade Union League to come in and help. A joint strike conference was organized and everyone pitched in.

Those were busy days for the members of the league. We organized a strike committee and set up all kinds of subcommittees to take care of the different problems. There was a committee on grievances; a picket committee of which Emma Steghagen was chairman; an organization committee under Agnes Nestor, who later took on the job of representing the league on the committee that paid out the commissary relief; a committee on publicity headed by Stella Franklin; and so on. We had strike headquarters at 275 La Salle Street, where we were close to the headquarters of many of the other labor organizations. Our biggest job was trying to relieve the distress of the strikers and their families. All the workers were so poor and had been able to save so little that they were continually in difficulties when they were out of work. Food, clothing, and coal had to be given to them. The gas company threatened to turn off the gas because the bills were not paid. Medical attention had to be secured for those who were ill. Then there was the problem of trying to keep up the morale of the strikers, many of whom were suffering terribly despite our efforts to help them.

There were dozens of meeting halls all over the city. Many different languages were used because the strikers were of different nationalities and often did not speak English. The biggest meetings were in Hodcarriers' Hall on the West Side. These meetings were always in an uproar. It was never possible to get order until one day a young man walked on the platform, rapped the gavel for order, and got it. He was Sidney Hillman, a cutter at Hart, Schaffner, and Marx. From that day on Hillman was chairman of the meetings at Hodcarriers' Hall and there was order. His talent for leadership asserted itself then and continued in the future. I saw much of him during the years immediately following the strike. We had many differences of opinion and at one time he was so angry with me he would not speak to me for three months, but our differences were always settled, and we remained good friends until his death.

We got very helpful publicity in most of the newspapers. I remember that Carl Sandburg, who was working for the *Daily News*, was one of the most helpful of the labor reporters. I knew him well in those days. He wrote splendid stories about the strike and the strikers. Sometimes we used to see him at small gatherings when he would play his banjo and sing and occasionally read his poetry. I always remember him as a friendly, understanding man and an accurate reporter who did not depend on sensational methods to get attention.

Finally, after the United Garment Workers had signed one agreement which was repudiated by the workers because it was just an agreement to go back to work, with no concessions and no hope for the future, an agreement for two years with the Hart, Schaffner, and Marx people was reached on January 14, 1910, by the United Garment Workers, the Chicago Federation of Labor, and the Chicago Women's Trade Union League. The most important feature of this agreement was that it recognized the right of the workers to strike and set up an arbitration committee with representatives of the employers and the workers to consider grievances.

After the Hart, Schaffner, and Marx agreement was reached the strike dragged on for another few weeks, during which time a number of other plants signed agreements and it looked as though victory was in sight. But suddenly on February 3 the strike was called off by the officials of the United Garment Workers without notifying John Fitzpatrick or Mrs.

Robins. This action resulted in much hard feeling between Mrs. Robins and the officials of the union. We were all disappointed and shocked. It was a "hunger bargain" for hundreds of workers who had suffered deeply during the strike and gained little when it was over.

But for many thousands it was a great victory. The right of collective bargaining had been recognized by the largest employer in the clothing industry and the machinery for arbitration was set up. For the Hart, Schaffner, and Marx Company an arbitration committee was appointed to adjust all grievances, with Carl Meyer representing the firm and W. O. Thompson representing the workers. The work of this committee was a practical and successful experiment in collective bargaining. It continued throughout the years ahead and became a model for the whole industry.

Another thing the workers gained from this strike was a feeling of solidarity. They realized after their experience that they must stand together if they were to get the things they needed.

I remember Mrs. Robins telling the story of the wife of a striker whom she visited. The woman was sick in bed, with several little children to take care of. Her husband had been asked three times by the firm to come back to work, but he had refused to desert the union. When Mrs. Robins asked how she could bear the hardships for her children, she replied, "We do not live only on bread. If I cannot give my children bread, I *can* give them liberty."

This is the spirit that is back of all the great struggles of the workers to improve their working conditions. Liberty and freedom for collective bargaining is what they want and it is what they must have.

5

Arbitration and Negotiation

ONE evening, after the strike was settled, I went to a meeting of the Women's Trade Union League. I had been working hard in the factory all day and I was tired after the many weeks of extra work connected with the strike. I wanted to let up and just float for a while. But I found that Mrs. Robins had other plans for me. She had been one of the signers of the Hart, Schaffner, and Marx agreement, because although the strikers had voted on the agreement and had accepted it, the firm said they wanted a guarantee of good behavior, so Mrs. Robins for the league and John Fitzpatrick for the Chicago Federation of Labor had signed it too. Mrs. Robins asked me to leave the factory and be the league's representative working with the United Garment Workers Union to carry out the terms of the agreement.

It was a hard decision to make. I did not know whether or not I would have any security in that kind of job. On the other hand, I was very anxious to quit the factory. The work was very hard and I did not make much money. The league offered to pay me eighteen dollars a week, which seemed like a big salary because in the factory I was only getting from eleven to fifteen dollars a week. Finally, after considering for a few days, I decided to make the change and I represented the league with the union for the next two years.

I have never regretted that decision. So far as doing something really constructive in the working world, I think that job on the Hart, Schaffner, and Marx agreement was the most important thing I have ever done.

All through that two years we had a turbulent time. Both sides had so much to learn. The firm had to learn how to deal with the workers through the union, and the workers had to learn how to keep their side of the agreement. There were plenty of difficulties.

In the first place, the superintendent of Hart, Schaffner, and Marx could never learn how to deal with the union. It had formerly been the practice in the factory if anyone complained of anything to take him by the neck and throw him out, and this superintendent could not learn anything different. Eventually, he left and a better superintendent came in.

Then, the firm hired a professor who was to be its labor representative. A good many problems came up because this professor took it upon himself to be both the firm and the union, and so tried to keep the union members from bringing up their grievances. He did not want to hear them at all, and until we got him educated, he did not realize that the only safety in the whole situation was the fact that the workers had the right to bring up their grievances. The result was that for about eighteen months there were strikes almost every day.

That is likely to happen with any young union. The workers had felt their power when they were all together during the strike. After they went back to work they were incensed when a grievance was not taken up promptly. They had not had the discipline of long union membership, so when they did not know just what to do, they would take the only action they knew of and go on strike. The arbitration method had been very little used, even by the older unions, and the members of the union were inexperienced and had not had time to learn to act through union representatives. They did not understand the delays in settling grievances; so when they got impatient they went on strike. It was our job to keep them from going out, to try to find out what their grievances were at the beginning and get them settled without strikes.

I worked till midnight nearly every day going to meetings and talking with the workers. Usually I would be called early in the morning and told to come down to the office quick because there was another bunch of workers down there on strike and I had to do something about it. They went out for all kinds of reasons. At first I, alone, and later with Bessie Abramowitz, one of the finishers at Hart, Schaffner, and Marx, who eventually became Mrs. Sidney Hillman, would go to the factories at noontime and when the workers came out for lunch we would walk around with them and talk to them about their grievances. We thought if we could get to them as early as that we would not have so many strikes. Then we would tell them about the evening meetings and ask them to come. In this way we were able to get some order and to stop some of the strikes, but we did not really accomplish much until after about a year, when we were able to persuade the workers to appoint chairmen in the different shops. These shop chairmen were better able to control the workers and keep them from striking while their grievances were being adjusted.

But we had one group of about six leaders of the pantsmakers' union that was always getting into trouble and striking. One day they went on strike for practically no reason at all. The impartial chairman for Hart, Schaffner, and Marx at that time was James Mullenbach. It was his responsibility to set all prices and settle all grievances. The firm paid half his salary and the union paid the other half. After hearing the story of the striking pantsmakers, Mr. Mullenbach ruled that the firm must take them back to work.

There was a great difference of opinion about this ruling. I personally felt that it was a mistake. We had only six months more until the agreement was over. The firm had all the justification in the world to say it would not sign a new agreement with this crowd. I thought we would have to stop strikes if we were ever to get a new agreement.

I met Mr. Mullenbach one day and found that he was uneasy about his decision. He asked me my opinion and I said I did not like it. He was disturbed. He went back to his office and later he called me up and said he did not know just what to do, but he thought something ought to be done. I suggested that he should talk it over with the arbitration committee. I said I would explain the situation to W. O. Thompson, the arbitration man for the union, Mr. Hillman, and John Fitzpatrick, president of the Chicago Federation of Labor.

Fitzpatrick, being much disturbed about the constant strikes, called a meeting of Thompson, Mrs. Robins, Hillman, and me. We waited and waited for Hillman to come, but he did not turn up until, after an hour, we called him again and urged him to come. We then told him we were going to recommend that the arbitration committee take over and reverse Mr. Mullenbach's decision. Hillman was so furious with me that he didn't speak to me for three months.

Following this, the arbitration committee had a meeting and fired the strikers. This broke up the pantsmakers' local, which was what Hillman had said would happen. However, a couple of months later, the workers who had been fired applied for jobs again and were taken back. Then they called a meeting of the pantsmakers and reorganized the local. Hillman was ill at the time and Bessie Abramowitz was helping to take care of him. She called me and said she had to attend a grievance committee meeting and asked if I would come up and look out for Hillman. I did, and he said when he saw me, "This is an awfully nice thing for you to do. I want to apologize. I didn't realize you could reorganize a local after it was once broken up. That was what I was concerned about."

This action of firing the men stopped the wildcat strikes, with the result that we got a much better agreement later when the first agreement expired.

My experience with the United Garment Workers Union and Hart, Schaffner, and Marx had a very great influence on my work in later years. I learned then the importance of sincere arbitration in labor disputes. I learned too the difficulties of educating both the workers and the employers to keep their bargain once an agreement is made.

In later years I have found that the public is apt to think that all a labor organization does is to strike and battle with the employers. This is not true. Strikes are what get into the newspapers. But the disputes and the grievances that are settled through peaceful negotiations are not given much publicity.

If people only knew more of the day-to-day adjustments that are made peacefully in many of the most important organized industries, they would be less antagonistic to the trade unions and would realize the constructive work that organized labor is doing to advance the cause of the workers, which is really the cause of all the people of the United States.

In July 1911, while I was working on the Hart, Schaffner, and Marx agreement, I wrote an editorial in *Life and Labor*, the magazine published by the Women's Trade Union League. This editorial expressed what I thought then and it is as true today as it was the day I wrote it. I said:

Our burdens are heavy in the day's work and seem distasteful to us but we are better off, both physically and morally, doing useful work than not working at all, and work under conditions of safety, short hours, and a living wage, is a good and a healthful life. We should so regard our honest calling as workers and demand that no one should gain a living without work.

Women workers do not organize as fast as they should. If the women who labor could only realize that the union movement means more to them than any other force! It means better wages and shorter hours. Better wages mean a home — a real home — and shorter hours mean family life, a life where father, mother and the children have time to be with one another and learn together and play together.

But the best part of the union is that it makes you think! And we working women have got to do some thinking. Long hours, working for barely enough to live on, make it hard to do any thinking! And the boss knows it. That is why he wants us to work long hours. If six million working women should really think, something would happen.

Even the women who escape from the factory by marriage can never be sure. Their husbands or they themselves may any time be obliged to work at factory labor and their wages and conditions will largely depend on the strength of the union.

Women workers do not understand arbitration as they should. I myself belong to an organization which has arbitration for its policy. The organization does not authorize the strike except as a last resource after every other means of bringing about a settlement has been tried and has failed.

As an illustration take the two cities of Lynn, Massachusetts, and Brockton, Massachusetts. Lynn is a city very poorly organized. Sometimes there is not a single organization there of any sort. Just at the present the situation is hardly more satisfactory, for though at this moment it is filled with unions, they are all the so-called independent unions, at odds with the national organization and its locals and therefore weak and unable to obtain material improvement in wages or conditions. There are constant disputes and strikes all the time. Under these conditions the workers fare badly. Few even of the married men among the shoemakers own a home. Not many can even afford to occupy a little flat, but they crowd with their wives and children into the boarding and rooming houses with which Lynn is filled.

Brockton on the other hand is well organized. Under the Boot and Shoe Workers' Union and its arbitration policy this city has had industrial peace for twelve years.

In our trade we have had a recent lesson as to the benefits of the trade union movement. Two thousand five hundred lasters in Brockton and vicinity obtained through the Boot and Shoe Workers' Union an advance in wages amounting to about $200,000 a year.

A New England Conference was formed about a year ago. They meet once a month. Our general officers meet with them all the time and for a year organizing and consulting has gone on.

Yet these results have been obtained in a trade only partly organized. What could not be expected if all boot and shoe makers were in the union?

Those days when I worked on the Hart, Schaffner, and Marx agreement were hard. My personal life was pretty much submerged. A typical day would begin about seven in the morning. I got my own breakfast, and ate with my sister, with whom I was living. About seven thirty I was usually called and told either that there was a strike on or that there was a committee meeting, at the Chicago Federation of Labor or the Women's Trade Union League office, at which a grievance was to be discussed. I would get to work at eight o'clock and spend all morning on these matters. Then I would go to the factories to see the workers as they came out. After that I would pick up lunch somewhere and go back either to our office or to the office of the union and have a committee meeting in the afternoon. Sometimes there were committee meetings right after people came out of the factory, between five and six o'clock.

Then we would try to get some dinner, followed usually by meetings in the evenings which ended any time between eight thirty and midnight. If I was on the West Side it would take three quarters of an hour to get home. But if the meeting was downtown, it would not take so long.

On weekends we did the same thing. On Sunday there was usually some kind of mass meeting. We would have speaking and sometimes we would have food. Then we often had dances on Sunday afternoons. The Chicago Federation of Labor and the Boot and Shoe Workers Union met on alternate Sunday afternoons.

Sunday mornings were free unless we had to distribute leaflets. I did not go to church myself. It was a hard schedule, particularly in winter, when it sleeted and snowed and was very cold. But I was strong and stood it all right.

One of the hardest things I had to learn was to be patient at a meeting when everyone had to make a speech and everyone else in turn condemned whatever suggestion was made and it sounded as if life depended on the subject they were discussing. You would know that these speeches were just something you had to get through so that you could go on, and in the end when the vote was taken it was usually unanimous.

I used to feel angry because of the waste of time and because of my anxiety to get things settled, but I finally got used to it.

A good deal of time is wasted at every labor meeting. To deal with labor, you have to be patient while everyone learns to work together. I think patience is one of the greatest disciplines in working with human beings. Intellectuals often fail in their relations with labor because they have no realization of the fight labor has had to put up. The laborer has had hard knocks and when he tries to get something he has to fight every step of the way. All his life has been a fight and he has not had time to spend on intellectual things and on the finer side of life. He has had to be a fighter to get things for his union. At first in our negotiations with Hart, Schaffner, and Marx even the conferences with the firm were fights in words. A union man would go in with a price list to the firm office and say, "If you don't do this by eleven o'clock we go on strike." The company officials would, of course, resent this attitude. And the fight would be on.

But gradually with more understanding and more experience these meetings turned into a question of wits, not a question of fighting, and those that could plead best won the day.

Nowadays, because the government itself has gathered so many facts on labor conditions, the labor leader has to be another kind of person. He has to be equipped to use facts and figures and be able to meet the high-powered legal representatives of the employers. The information he needs he can usually get from the government, but this was not the case in the early days. Facts gathered by an impartial organization were not available and all the information a representative of labor could get came from the workers themselves. But this information was inadequate and had little meaning, so the labor leader had to rely mostly on his wits.

6

The Organizer at Work

AFTER the termination of the first Hart, Schaffner, and Marx agreement and the signing of a new one in 1913, better arbitration machinery was developed and I was no longer needed to work with the unions. I was kept on as general organizer for the Chicago Trade Union League and later for the national league. I worked in all sorts of other league activities too. In fact, during the next four years, from 1913 to 1917, I was immersed in the problems of women workers and the firsthand experience I gained then was a great help in later years when I had to deal with the same problems on a national scale.

I still lived with my sister Anna, whose husband had died some time before, on the North Side, but I was so busy with my work in the league that I did not spend much time at home. However, the work was easier than it had been. I did not have to get to the office until ten or eleven in the morning and the Sunday work was not quite as strenuous. Of course, there were still the Boot and Shoe Workers Union and the Chicago Federation of Labor meetings, but they were over earlier and on Sunday evenings I was glad to be home. Sometimes we had a few of my friends over on Sunday evenings and sometimes I would go to their houses. We would sit and sing, mostly Irish songs because many of the girls were Irish.

It was nice not to have to go to a meeting every moment of the day.

My first job in the new work for the national league was to go to Philadelphia and help in organizing the girls in the garment workers industry. Most of the girls in the trade were Jewish and were organized in the International Ladies Garment Workers Union, but they were not able to impress the other girls with the need for organizing.

There was talk against unions all over the country because the employers, as well as the public, thought that belonging to a union, particularly a union dominated by immigrants, was a stigma. Many girls felt that it was below their dignity to belong to such a trade union.

We had a local Women's Trade Union League in Philadelphia at that time. Its organizer was Myrtle Whitehead, who had previously worked in a factory in Baltimore. Together, she and I tried to organize these girls. We would get their names from the Jewish girls and would ask them to one of the settlements, where we would have coffee and sandwiches and cake to entice them to come. We were fairly successful, but the work had its ups and downs for a year before they became organized and stayed organized.

After three or four months in Philadelphia, I was called back to Chicago to do organization work there. Our greatest difficulty there was that the opposition of the employers was so severe that the leaders in the trade unions did not feel they were strong enough to meet it. Also, the times were not very good, a great many people were out of work, and those who had jobs had to be very careful so that they would not lose them. Therefore, they hesitated to belong to a union or to take leadership if they did belong.

In a great many cases the organization of the union would come after the workers went out on strike, because then they were all out together and their strength came only by staying together. If they were to get any recognition from the firms in settling the strike, they had to stick together. Besides that, they were always in dire need and it was necessary to have relief, otherwise they would have to go back to work. Organization was necessary for this, too. Of course, we tried to get them organized without striking but it was not always possible.

The strikes usually started because of intolerable conditions in the industry. The chief reason was the very low wages that were prevalent, but the long hours, overtime without extra pay, unfair systems of fines, and unsanitary working conditions also played their part in arousing the workers to protest in the only way they knew to be effective, by striking.

Once a strike started, picketing was carried on under very great difficulties. The first thing that a firm would do was to go before a judge and get an injunction against everything that could possibly be connected with a strike. Picketing, even walking within a certain distance of the factory, would be included in the injunction. Police were always stationed at the plant and they were not always gentle with the strikers.

During one strike of the garment workers, there were many arrests. I was asked by the union and also detailed by the league to get bail for the strikers. This was very hard to do, because the bail required was four hundred dollars for each girl arrested. The police stations in the city were notoriously bad — the sanitary conditions were awful and the cells in the basement were regular dungeons — so we had to do everything we could to get the girls out.

One day about seven in the morning I went to the Des Plaines Street station. Five girls were sitting in the dungeons. I called up Mrs. Mary Wilmarth, a member of one of the older families in Chicago and mother of the first Mrs. Harold Ickes. She lived at the Congress Hotel and owned the ground it was built on. She was a beautiful and fine person, reminding me of "lavender and old lace." A member of the league, she was a real friend of labor.

While I waited for her to come, I went down to visit the girls. I knew that they had had no breakfast and it was a cold

Matilda and Magnus Anderson, Mary Anderson's parents

Mary Anderson's childhood home near Lidköping, Sweden

Mary Anderson, upper left, with fellow members of the Boot and Shoe Workers Union in Chicago, about 1912; Emma Steghagen, second from right, back row, later became a leader in the National Women's Trade Union League

Mary McDowell   *Mrs. Raymond Robins*

Successive presidents of the Chicago Women's Trade Union League

Agnes Nestor

John Fitzpatrick

Victor Olander

Chicago labor leaders in the World War I period

Mary Anderson

Edward N. Nockles

morning. I went out to get some coffee and doughnuts for them and while I was away Mrs. Wilmarth came and I missed her. When I got back I went to the clerk, who said she had been there and gone; he would not tell me anything more, but I knew she had not deserted us. Soon she came in with Judge John McGoorty, an old friend of hers. She said the clerk at the jail would not believe her when she put up as collateral the ground on which the Congress Hotel was built, so she got Judge McGoorty and brought him over. The clerk was finally convinced and accepted the collateral, and the girls were liberated.

Mrs. Samuel Dauchy was another of the allies of the league who was always helpful in bailing out the girls; so too was Mrs. Frank R. Lillie, wife of a professor at Chicago University and a member of the Crane family. One day Mrs. Lillie came down to give bail and put up some property as security. The clerk said, "What is the value of the property you own?" She answered, "Oh, a million or more." The clerk was dumbfounded, but it was true and she helped us many times.

I myself was arrested once during this strike and I will always remember my feeling of defilement, both physical and spiritual, after I got out of that cell. In order to keep in touch with the picketers and find out when they were arrested, I was waiting about two blocks away from the picket line when one of the picketers came rushing up to me with the news that several of them were being arrested. We started together for the nearest drugstore where there was a telephone and just as we got to the drugstore I felt a hand on my shoulder and heard a gruff voice say, "You are under arrest."

It was a policeman who had followed the girl bringing me the message. When I asked why I was arrested and said I had done nothing and had not been in the picket line, the answer was just "Shut up! You are under arrest." He refused to let me telephone to the office of the league to tell them what had happened and made us walk with him to the Des Plaines Street police station. About six of the girls who had been picketing were there too. They had been arrested because one of them had yelled "scab" at an automobile load of strikebreakers that the company had driven into the plant. The police refused to let us telephone for help and put us right into the cells.

I was alone in a filthy cell with nothing in it except a dirty old cot and a wooden chair. The cell had an open sewer running through it and the smell was disgusting. After about an hour a guard came and said if I would give him the telephone number he would send my message for me, so I gave him the directions and he went off.

About two hours later we were all let out of the cells and taken to court. The league had called Harold Ickes' office for help and he sent Donald Richberg down to defend me. After a short discussion between Mr. Richberg and the judge, we were all dismissed, and I went home and took a bath and changed my clothes, but I did not get rid of the feeling of dirt and defilement for a long time afterward.

Shortly after the garment strike was over, we had a strike of waitresses. At the Henrici restaurant, which was noted for good food and for its large clientele, a picket line was established. The picketers were treated very badly. They would go on about eleven thirty in the morning at the corner of Dearborn and Washington streets, one of the busiest corners in the city. Thousands of people would assemble there about that time. The police were very tough; they yanked the arm of one girl out of its socket and another girl had her arm broken.

Ellen Gates Starr, who established Hull House with Jane Addams, came down to me one morning and said, "What can I do to help?" I said, "I wish you would go to the picket line and see that the girls get better treatment. I'll be along later."

She went off and when I arrived a little while later, I could not get through the crowd. Some of the newspapermen were taking pictures from the lamp posts. I elbowed my way through and there stood little Miss Starr with a big policeman holding her arm. I asked what was the matter and the policeman said, "If you don't shut up, I'll arrest you too."

When they were arrested, the girls would not walk over to the police station. The police had to get the patrol wagon. Then when the girls were put into the wagon they would make speeches from the back. We would follow them to the station house after telephoning one of our friends, Mrs. Wilmarth, Mrs. Dauchy, Mrs. Ickes, or one of the others, who would be there waiting for us to come in and would bail them out. If the girls were not bailed out immediately, they were carted to another police station where there were cells and locked up.

Miss Starr was bailed out immediately. She had said that she had a right to walk on that sidewalk as an American citizen. We knew there had to be a test case for illegal arrest in this situation and we decided that Miss Starr was a good person to make it. A jury trial was held. The man who was the prosecutor for the city lived at Hull House and Miss Starr was a good friend of his, so it was a difficult situation for him. Of course, the prosecution did not have a case against anyone and Miss Starr was let off very quickly.

After that strike petered out there was another strike in a chain of restaurants owned by a German who spoke broken English. Elizabeth Maloney was the business agent of the waitresses at that time. This man had great respect for her. When we had a jury trial of some of the strikers, he took the stand. He was a very profane man and every once in a while he would start swearing and his attorney would interrupt, "You mustn't talk that way," but the judge said, "Let him tell it his own way." At one point the lawyer asked, "What did you do the morning of the strike?" and the witness replied, "Vy ve didn't haf anyding to eat. I couldn't ged anyding. I couldn't ged more than two dozen doughnuts any place. Isn't that so, Miss Maloney?" Elizabeth backed up his statement and we were pleased to find that we had had that much support for the strike.

Then the women in a broom factory went out on strike. It was a very severe strike because the manufacturer had a foreman who did not stop at anything. He sometimes slugged the workers if they had a disagreement at work. I went to talk with the employer and he said I did not know how terrible these girls were. "They're a lot of immigrants and they carry knives in their pockets." I asked him why they did this and he said they had them to slug people with when they were on the picket line. I asked him if they had ever done that and he replied, "No, not yet." I told him that I had heard stories about one of his foremen, not only of his brutality in dealing with the women but also that he was immoral and that immoral conditions existed in the plant because of him. The employer said he knew this was so and I suggested that perhaps the girls carried knives because of it. The employer would not agree at first, but finally the strike was settled, the foreman was fired, and the wages were raised a little.

About a year after I started organizing work for the league, we heard that the miners in the spar mines in Hardin County were on strike and were in a terrible plight. Some of the miners came to Chicago and asked the Women's Trade Union League for help because they were being evicted from their homes. Since so little was known about the strike, Mrs. Robins thought we should investigate it and asked Agnes Burns, William Holly, the attorney for the league and a well-known liberal, and me to go down and find out what the facts were.

Since there were no trains into Hardin County, we went by boat on the Mississippi River to a little town where we had to spend the night. We could not go to a hotel because the hotel was against the striking miners, so we stayed at a little boardinghouse and ate one meal at a store and another at a miner's house. The food was very bad.

The next day we went to Rosiclare, where the miners were, and stayed with one of the engineers who had asked us to come down. We found the situation there was very tense. The conditions for the miners were awful. Their homes were just huts, one little room, sometimes a chair and sometimes not, a table, a stove, and a few cooking utensils. But they were being evicted from even these meager accommodations. Their poverty and misery were dreadful to see. The spirit in the town was very bitter. In the evening when we sat on the porch talking, about fifteen mine guards paraded back and forth in front of the house trying to frighten us. Our host said his garden was the only safe place for us to have a meeting, so the next morning we went around to the miners' houses and told them we would have a meeting there. Later on when a rumor went around that we had left town because we were scared and that there would be no meeting, we had to walk around the town to show that we were there.

As the time arrived for the meeting about fifty mine guards with guns pointed at us surrounded the garden. When we asked them why they were there, they said, "There'll be a riot." I said, "Who's going to riot? Not the miners!" They replied that the men who were working below ground in the mines (scabs) would come up. My answer was that they wouldn't come up at two o'clock in the afternoon unless they were asked to do so by the company or by the guards. Then the sheriff came and asked me what I was going to say; I told him to come in and listen. He did and had to sit with the miners, which he did not like much.

In my speech I did not say anything about the company, but told the miners they were entitled to a living wage and that there should be arbitration between the company and the men. Agnes spoke too, telling about her early life in a mining village. She was a miner's daughter and we wanted them to understand that we really knew what we were talking about. Afterward the sheriff said, "If everyone talked like that, there wouldn't be any trouble!"

The mayor of the town was in the crowd. He was sympathetic to the miners and because of his attitude, the mine guards would often kidnap him. When this meeting was over we were afraid he would get into trouble because one of the guards ran up and slapped him in the face, but he just sat down and there was no riot.

Finally, the women who had come to the town with the scabs came along. They lined up, watching us and calling us names. As they came closer and closer, I went out to them and said they must understand that there was no difference of opinion between us, that we were all working for better conditions for the workers. After that they left.

We were having coffee and coffee cake before taking the boat, which was to leave at four o'clock, when word came that the men who had been brought in to take the places of the striking miners were going to hiss us out of town. In order to avoid this, because we did not want to start a riot, I asked for and got an automobile. We took the mayor along with us to the next town where we met Mr. Holly, who had been helping defend some arrested miners. There we left the mayor and started our trip back to Chicago.

This was my first experience with the bitter feeling that existed in these mining communities, and with the terrible conditions under which the miners lived in a "company" town. When we reported the facts, on our return to Chicago, we were able to get some publicity about them. Eventually the coal miners' union took over and conditions were improved.

Later on I had another experience with a mine strike in the copper mines of northern Michigan. The conditions there were very much like those at Rosiclare except for the fact that it was winter and the situation was much worse. I saw there again the evils of a "company" town and the terrible power it gives to an employer to be able to control not only the working conditions but the entire lives of his workers.

The work in the mines was very hazardous. The miners had to go down into the bowels of the earth to work where the temperature was very high. Then they would come up at the end of the day into snow and below-zero weather. The pay was very small.

The miners had been on strike for quite a while. They were not allowed on the mine owner's property, which included most of the town. They could not go to the post office to get their mail. Their houses were on the mine owner's property and they were being evicted. Some were living in hastily constructed shacks. They could not get any food in the store and because they were out in the hills where the mines were and away from any city, there was no other place to get supplies. Besides all that, they had no money.

After I got back to Chicago and reported the situation, there was quite a bit of negotiation in which the league took part and finally the strike was settled and conditions were somewhat improved the following year, because the United Mine Workers Union had become aware of the situation through our reports and the spar miners were included in the state legislation that had been passed some years before to regulate conditions for the coal miners.

Another difficult job we had was organizing state employees, particularly in the state institutions for the insane. The work of the attendants in these institutions was very hard. There was no limit to their hours and the pay was only thirty dollars a month, with maintenance.

The institutions were scattered all over Illinois and I went from one to the other and organized the attendants. We were finally able to get from the State Board for Institutions regulations establishing the eight-hour day and a substantial increase in pay.

During that time, the first institution I organized was at Dunning, just outside of Chicago. I got along very well with the members for a considerable time and then one man objected to my coming out and telling them what to do. He made a fuss about it one night at a union meeting and as the other members did not defend me, I thought it was probably time for me to withdraw.

Shortly afterward, the president of the local came to see me and begged me to come back to their meetings. He said members were dropping out. I had so much to do in down-state Illinois that I did not get there for some time. In the meantime, they organized a mass meeting in the big hall of the institution and asked Mr. Holly and me to come out to speak. As I was sitting on the platform during this meeting the same man who had made the fuss sat next to me. He began to act queerly and some of the nurses moved over right away. First he took off his shoes and then put them on again when the nurses told him to. I began to realize, then, that he was now one of the inmates.

Mr. Holly was speaking and was embarrassed because the people in the audience were laughing and he could not understand what they were laughing about, not knowing what was going on behind him. The nurses were apprehensive that the man would do me some harm, so they stayed near and kept their eyes on him every moment, much to the interest of the audience. Nothing happened, however, and after the meeting Mr. Holly was relieved to find that the audience had not been laughing at him. The man had been an attendant, but had gone insane on the job. All of which goes to show that you never know what you will come up against when you are doing organizational work!

7

Women in Trade Unions

SHORTLY after I had been up in the mining district of northern Michigan the time came for me to take my citizenship examination. It was 1915, twenty-seven years after I had entered the United States. I really got interested in becoming a citizen because there was a great stir in Illinois at that time about giving suffrage to women. If women were going to get the vote I wanted to have it too, so I decided to get my final papers. I had taken out my first papers a long time before, but I could not become a citizen until I was examined and I had to have witnesses to vouch for me.

When I came before the examiner I was very nervous, not knowing what he was going to ask me. It was not a very impressive occasion. The examiner sat at a regular desk and I and my witnesses, one of whom was Emma Steghagen, sat before him and answered his questions. I remember he asked me who was governor of Illinois, who was President of the United States, and who was secretary of labor. Of course, I knew the right answers and when he asked me if I knew who was the assistant secretary of labor I said, "Yes, Mr. Louis Post, who is a very good friend of mine." I think this rather surprised him because he stopped asking me questions then and called on Emma Steghagen.

During Emma's examination about me she happened to

mention that I had recently been in the copper mine district in Michigan. That seemed to make the examiner suspicious; he called me back and asked if I was a socialist. I said No, and then he asked if I had not carried a red socialist flag when I was up in the mines. I replied that there had not been any marching while I was there. After a few more questions he let me go. A few days later I appeared before the court and the judge only asked me if I had read the Constitution of the United States. When I answered Yes he directed that I be given my citizenship papers.

This was the first time that I had been openly accused of being a socialist, but in later years I became accustomed to being included in most of the lists of socialists, labor agitators, and finally communists, or "reds," that were made up by the reactionaries who were opposing labor legislation and trade union organization. It did not bother me then, and it never did later on except when I was accused of using my official position in the federal government to further communist programs. Then I felt that I had a responsibility to the American people to see that these statements were withdrawn because they could affect the work I was trying to do. But as far as I was concerned personally, I always thought that actions spoke louder than words and if people could oppose me only by saying I was a socialist or a communist their opposition was not very important.

In my day, I have received plenty of criticism, but I have not minded it. In fact, some of it has been very helpful and the rest I have always felt was made by people who did not know all the facts and so it was not worth worrying about. I always did whatever job I had to do as well as I could under the circumstances and I never found that it was any help to anyone to get upset if things did not come out exactly as I had wanted them to. I think my work in trade union organizing and arbitration taught me not to expect too much and to be satisfied with part of a cake if I could not get a whole one.

One of our problems with some of the early trade union

women was that they were not satisfied with what they could get. They became so enthusiastic about what they thought they could do that the first thing we knew we had some small prima donnas on our hands and this had its effect on their usefulness. I remember one girl who was working with the garment workers when there was a strike in a corset factory in Kalamazoo, Michigan. She was in charge of the strike and had such exalted ideas of herself that she thought she could lead a revolution. The result was that the firm secured an injunction against her and she got thirty days in jail. When she had served her time she came back to Chicago and quit her job.

Later, when the waitresses were on strike and there was an injunction against picketing, one of the girls came to me and said, "I'm going to defy the injunction and picket that restaurant because I know that if I do the workers will rise up in protest against the whole situation." My answer was, "That is what that girl in Kalamazoo thought, and she served thirty days in jail. The same thing would happen to you and nothing would be accomplished." I kept her from defying the injunction and we got a settlement by arbitration.

Another thing I learned during the years I was organizing was that to get women into the trade union movement required a technique that was different from organizing men. From the very beginning, I myself worked with men very successfully both in the factory and in the trade union movement, but I appreciated the difficulties that women met with, and I knew that in general they should have different treatment than men.

My first experience of being the only woman official among men officials came when I was on the executive board of the Boot and Shoe Workers Union. There were eleven members and I was the only woman. Because our president and secretary were such fine men, I had no great difficulties. But one thing that was very conspicuous to me then and has always remained in my mind since is how very petty men can be to one another, even among really superior people, as I felt most of those men were. I suppose because I was the only woman, they would come to me with their little grievances among themselves, talking about this one and that one. I have always felt since that experience that the talked-about pettiness of women to one another has its counterpart among men. I think it is probably just human nature. I knew these men very well and they accepted me as one of them. I went to every meeting and social gathering and was never embarrassed. It was very heartening but it did not follow through in my experience after that.

In my official position in the government, I found that we constantly had to call the men's attention to the fact that women should be represented on committees and in any kind of official gathering. Sometimes they included us and sometimes they did not. I always felt the men considered government as a man's business and did not want woman's intrusion there. Even if it was necessary to take up the question of women's employment and conditions of life the men never felt that a woman could speak for women.

I found, too, that there was a great tendency among government officials, particularly during World War II, to speak about "the people" as a whole, but when they spoke of "the people" they meant the men. Some of the women thought that they got personal recognition, saying, "I never have any trouble working with men," because they were consulted now and then and that was sufficient for them. It was not sufficient for me.

In the early days I was fighting for the women in the trade union movement. Some men did not want to organize women because they felt that the women were competitors. Because women were paid less, the men believed that if they excluded women they had won the day. It was the same sort of attitude that the trade unionists had in the early days about the improvement of machinery. Instead of trying to improve the machines, they tried to exclude them. Those fights against women and against improved machinery went on for many

years and are still going on to a certain extent. But it was really
the improvement of conditions that should have been looked
after instead of wasting time opposing progress.

My ambition was to get better working conditions — and
that included better wages — for women. I had found personally that it was very hard to live on the little we earned and
I knew we could not do anything or get anywhere unless we
were all together. The thing I had always worried about was
what would become of me when I was not able to work in
the factory any longer, and I think that idea permeated the
thoughts of all the people in the factory. We were never able
to get ahead and it was a great struggle to keep within what
we made and eke out a living. Yet we felt that we must get
ahead and make what we had a little better. It was a question
of security then just as it is today.

A good many girls expected to settle the question of their
future by getting married. But that did not always work because they might marry a worker who did not have a secure
wage. Then, after children came, the whole family would
have to try to live on that wage. If they were asked to join
the union some girls would say, "Well, I don't care, I'm not
going to work in a factory all my life. I'm going to get married." Their great ambition was to get out of the factory.
They thought that would take care of them and did not realize
that many other responsibilities would rest upon them in later
years.

I thought, as a young girl, that I would get married too, but
somewhere I lost myself in my work and never felt that marriage would give me the security I wanted. I thought that
through the trade union movement we working women could
get better conditions and security of mind.

The question of marriage is very important in the organization of women, and of men too, for that matter. Underlying
the whole situation is the need for security in employment
and sufficient wages to permit some saving. To a certain extent, the social security allotments do this now. It is a small

security but it is a beginning and a beginning in the right direction. But in the days when I was organizing, the only security women could see was in marriage and that made it difficult to get many of them into the trade union movement. When they once are inducted into a union, however, and become interested, I think women are just as good members as men are, and sometimes better.

We did everything we could to interest women in the unions, developing special techniques that were very helpful. In the first place, we found that we had to get nice places for the girls to meet in. The men met in halls that were often back of a saloon, or in questionable districts, dirty and not well kept. I remember the so-called labor temples that were anything but temples. The girls would not go to meetings in these places and we could not ask them to go under the circumstances. Then, when it came to paying dues at the headquarters of the union, the girls found it very distasteful to go where there were large groups of men playing cards and hanging about. In well-organized unions, of course, the dues were collected in the factories or some place near by, but most of the unions in which we were organizing in those days had not set up this system of dues collection.

To eliminate this problem we tried to get nice places for the girls to meet in order to lure them to come. Girls and women like a homelike atmosphere and a social get-together now and then. They get tired of just talking about conditions of work in the factory. So every other meeting we used to try and arrange for some kind of social gathering. Sometimes we would serve coffee or tea and cakes. It was not easy for us to do this. We had no money, we were tired after the day's work, and it was an added burden to make the preparation and to clear up afterward, but it helped and we were probably more successful in our work with women because of it.

Of course, we tried different things with different groups. I remember especially one time when we arranged with the Ward-Corby bakery to let us take groups of girls to visit their place. It was a big and beautiful plant and when we got through our tour the bakery would serve a delicious snack. It was an educational tour and nutritious too, and was a fine break for the girls.

We especially tried to organize the industries in Chicago where women predominated. One of our campaigns was among the clerks in the department stores. Their working conditions were poor but the wages were poorer yet. A great many women were getting only five to six dollars a week. That was particularly true of the best stores. In the stores where the goods were not so expensive, there was a greater turnover and the girls made more money because they got, in addition to their weekly wages, a percentage on sales. The better class of stores, with less turnover, were supposed to compensate their clerks by giving them a steady and more agreeable job, but they did not do it.

To start the campaign, we called a meeting and were finally successful in persuading a number of the girls to come to it. We were not able, however, to get any publicity. None of the papers would publish a story and we felt that unless there was publicity so that the girls would know what was going on, we would not be very successful.

While we were puzzling over this problem, Mrs. Medill McCormick offered to come and speak at one of the meetings. We were delighted, for we knew that if she spoke the *Tribune*, which was owned by the McCormicks, would carry a story. Mrs. McCormick was a great friend of ours. Daughter of a famous senator, Mark Hanna, and wife of Medill McCormick, who was becoming a political power in Illinois, she had great political sense and a good deal of influence. Tall, slender, and full of vitality, she would make, we knew, a vigorous speech that would arouse the enthusiasm of the meeting. Our hopes were high when the meeting opened and she began to speak. But she was feeling ill, and just as she started she fainted and we had to send her home.

I talked to her the next day on the telephone and she said,

"I have never done such a foolish thing in my life before and I don't know why I should have fainted. But there is one compensation, and that is that you got your publicity." In spite of the story we got in the papers, however, our campaign with the store clerks was not successful, partly because there was a very weak international union. There was also tremendous opposition from the owners of the stores and the papers carried other very unfavorable stories because the owners demanded it and the papers wanted their advertisements.

One of our great problems in organizing women was to get in touch with them and let them know there was an organization they could turn to if they wanted to improve their conditions of work. I remember what trouble we had when we tried to organize the candy industry. It was a very seasonal industry in those days because there was not the general refrigeration that we have now, and much of the candy could not be made in hot weather but had to be made in the season, which lasted only about six months of the year. All summer there was almost no work, but there was generally a great spurt before the holidays and at Easter time. The candy workers were mostly immigrants. One season we were able to organize them and got an eight-hour day and a small increase in wages, but the next season when the factories reopened there was an entirely new set of people and we had to begin all over again.

The men in this trade were not organized either, so we started out to organize them too. First we tried to get acquainted in some way with a few of the workers. We met them through other organizations and through any of their relatives that we knew. We would talk things over with a few of them and find out about the conditions of their employment. Then we had this information printed on leaflets, which we distributed at the factory gates when the workers were coming out. A few days later we would distribute another leaflet calling a meeting and urging them to come. We were not always successful, maybe no one would come to the meetings, but when their next problem came up the workers would know where to go and we would help them and get them interested in that way.

We would also get hold of some of them when they complained to us about the violations of the labor laws. When they became more interested, we had one hundred thousand leaflets printed in five languages stating the law and the worker's rights under the law. Sometimes we would go to the early morning church services, particularly the Catholic ones, because we knew that the workers would have to go to early Mass in order to get to work on time. As they came out from the service we would distribute the leaflets to them. I think probably we were able to acquaint the workers with the law better in that way than in any other. At the bottom of the leaflet was the telephone number to call if the law was violated, our address, and that of the Labor Department. They were urged to call and report violations and we guaranteed that no names would be used by us or by the Department of Labor. When reports came in we turned them over to the Labor Department. Its officials investigated and if the employers could not be persuaded to desist they were brought into court and fined.

All this helped in getting people into the union, but of course the greatest inducement was to negotiate through the union and get an increase in pay. When we did that the workers really appreciated what a union could do, and they were ready to join.

Just after we went into World War I, when the second stockyards organization campaign was carried on by a combination of several unions, including the engineers' union, the Women's Trade Union League, the Chicago Federation of Labor, and a number of others, I tried to organize the miscellaneous workers.

I lived way out on the North Side and had to go to the South Side to distribute leaflets and try to get people to come to meetings. I was not too successful. At the meetings sometimes there would be one person, sometimes two. The next morning at the office they would ask me if I had been able to organize the people at the meeting and I would say, "Yes, I organized them one hundred per cent." We had better attendance at the Sunday meetings. One time we had a hall full of colored men and a few colored women. They got very "het up" over the union, and some of the newly organized men suggested it would be a good idea for strengthening the union if we could get an increase in wages for those who belonged to the union and not for the others! As a result of the arbitration that followed the organization campaign, Judge Samuel Alschuler, who was the arbitrator, gave the eight-hour day and an increase in wages. After that we could not get halls big enough for our meetings.

In the trade union movement, as in a good many other cases, "nothing succeeds like success." The hardest work is done by the pioneers and that is what we were in those early days in Chicago.

8

Working for Legislation

ALL the time that we were working in Chicago to organize women we were also working in Springfield trying to get some kind of labor legislation limiting hours of work for women.

I felt very strongly about getting legislation because the trade unions were not very powerful and we had all we could do to settle wage disputes. Our main work in the unions was the setting of prices for piecework and we could do very little about hours. There was no doubt in anyone's mind about the need for shorter hours, especially for women. The ten hours in the factory, plus the time needed to get there and home again, did not leave any extra time for all the work at home that is almost invariably the woman's responsibility. It was bad for health and very bad for family life to have the women so worn out at the end of a day's work that they had no strength or energy left for anything else. I felt that under the circumstances laws putting a limit to women's working hours were the only way we could improve these conditions and I was glad to join with the others when they were working for legislation.

I never found that special hour restrictions for women were any handicap to them. In the shoe factories where I worked, the men came in to work at seven and the women did not come in until seven thirty. In spite of this there was no feeling among the men against the special regulations for the women in my trade, or so far as I know, in other trades.

The Women's Trade Union League for many years was the spearhead in the fight for hour legislation for women in Illinois. Agnes Nestor was one of the leaders in this movement and she stuck at it for years until finally in 1937 the eight-hour law was passed.

I did not spend a great deal of time on legislation, because I was busy organizing, but sometimes in an emergency I would go to Springfield when the legislature was in session and work with the others.

One year, when Medill McCormick was a member of the legislature, he wanted to introduce a bill establishing an eight-hour day for women. We were not anxious for him to do this because we thought there was no chance for it to pass, but he introduced it just the same, so we had to go to work for it.

Those of us who were working for legislation lived in Springfield for several weeks. It was a very interesting time. Mrs. McCormick was there working for the child labor bill and there were many liberal people working for other things who were very helpful. Eventually, in spite of the fact that we were not sure of our support in the legislature, Mr. McCormick called up the bill.

As always, some of the men got up on the floor and made sarcastic speeches to defeat the bill, saying that their wives were working more than eight hours a day and they wanted them included in the bill. Finally one of our friends said that he did not consider his wife a servant to him, that her working hours were not comparable with those of a woman who was employed to do a certain job and had no control over its conditions, and that the opposition was talking nonsense. In the end, the bill came up for a vote and was defeated, in spite of some support.

Another time we could not get our bill out of the committee. At the time there was an election going on in Chicago for mayor and for aldermen. One of the members of the committee from the stockyards district, who was a union man, was home electioneering for himself for alderman. He returned to Springfield to vote and helped keep the bill from being reported out of the committee.

On our way home, we were on the train with Mr. McCormick and he said he would put up the money if we would defeat that man from the stockyards. In Chicago we called together a large number of union waitresses, who were especially interested in hour legislation, and got a wagon for them to go about in. Some of the girls were Polish and made speeches in Polish to the stockyards workers. They rode through the stockyards for two days before the election and we defeated the fellow.

Later, at the next session of the legislature, we heard some of the legislators saying, "Do you know what the girls did? They defeated him!" The defeated candidate for alderman came to us during the session and said, "Now girls, what do you want? I know what you did to me." After that he was with us and worked for us.

In all our work for legislation we had a good deal of help from the unions. John Fitzpatrick, president of the Chicago Federation of Labor, was always with us and we worked closely together. Another man who was a great help was Victor Olander, secretary-treasurer of the State Federation of Labor. Olander had been a seaman on the Great Lakes. He was a tall, blond, handsome man and had a very good legal mind which was especially valuable in the work of the state federation, so much of which dealt with legislation. He was one of the labor leaders who was always a helpful friend of the Women's Trade Union League and was understanding of our problems. We used to confer with Fitzpatrick and Olander when there was to be a session of the legislature and decide what legislation the Chicago and the State Federation of Labor would support and in what order. Usually, the bills we were sponsoring came second or third, but when the eight-hour law was put through it was the first bill to be brought up.

But, although we had the official sympathy and cooperation of the men's unions, sometimes we had to break down prejudices of individual members. I remember at one American Federation of Labor convention the question came up of indorsing the eight-hour day for women. Andrew Furuseth of the seamen's union spoke against it. Furuseth was one of the most picturesque of the labor leaders. Tall and lean with a lined, weather-beaten face, he looked like an angry eagle when he took the floor in opposition. He was a bachelor, and he spoke against the resolution because of his chivalrous attitude, and in his honesty I think he really believed it, that women belonged in the home and that men should take care of them.

Melinda Scott was at the convention and she asked for the floor to answer him. Melinda was a hat worker who had immigrated to this country from England. She was a very fiery little person and spoke with a strong English accent. She had worked in a factory in England when she was a child and because she was so very small she used to be shown as an exhibit of what child labor did to people. Actually, I doubt if that was the reason for her smallness. She was perfectly healthy and strong and I imagine her size was just a natural condition. Anyway, when she started to answer Furuseth, Mr. Gompers, who was presiding, asked her to get up on the table so the delegates could see her. From that exalted position Melinda launched out at Furuseth, and ended by saying, "If the men are taking care of the women, I want to know how many women Mr. Furuseth has taken care of." Furuseth was very much upset by this question. It must have made an impression on him, because later on, after he had thought things over, he changed his mind and went along with us.

This kind of prejudice and sentimentality about working women is one of the things we have had to combat all through the years. "Woman's place is in the home" sounds like a fine slogan but it is completely false when you come to examine the real conditions. Everyone who knows anything about working women knows that they work to support themselves and to contribute to the support of their families. They do not do it for "pin money" or for fun. There was not much "fun" in a ten-hour day of factory work and there was not much "pin money" either after the week's pay had been spread over the expenses of living. I myself, although I suppose most people thought I was a single woman without family responsibilities, turned over my pay envelope to my sister as long as I was living with her. She would give me back what we thought I needed. After I stopped living with her, I still made regular contributions to her support, and eventually, when she came to live with me, household expenses were my responsibility.

Over a period of thirty years in connection with any legislation for women we have had to hammer away at this prejudice and I am not sure that we have cleared it up yet. Sometimes the old pin money and women's place is in the home theories crop up even now to defeat progressive measures for enlarging women's opportunities.

Another of the difficulties we had to face in planning hour legislation for women was the problem of suiting the legislation to the special requirements of certain jobs. For instance, the waitresses presented a very difficult problem. Even if they worked a ten-hour day, their work was intermittent and spread over a longer period. There was not much they could do in the free time between working periods. They could not stay downtown and go to the movies and stores all the time. If they went home it meant triple car fare and most of their free time would be spent on the streetcars. In formulating legislation to limit their hours of work the thing that bothered us most was deciding how to get a reasonable day's work within a reasonable over-all period. Eight hours of actual working time within an over-all period of ten or eleven hours was the final solution and worked very well. In order to give the girls a place to rest when they were off duty, the Women's Trade Union League set up a rest room in the downtown district. For some time my sister, Anna Lind, was in charge of this room, which was open until five o'clock in the afternoon. It was a nice room with a few beds and some easy chairs and the girls could rest or sit and talk and sew until it was time for them to go back to work again.

When we were in Springfield working for hour legislation for the waitresses it was interesting to see how much more sympathetic the legislators were if they could actually visualize the job and knew some of the women who were doing the work they were discussing. Elizabeth Maloney, who was a member of the league and of the waitresses' union, waited on table in a downtown restaurant where a great many of the legislators took their meals when they were in Chicago. They knew her and liked her, so when she went to Springfield she always had friends there. When they were discussing the bill they would say, "Well, there's a waitress here now who is for this bill. I know what her work is like because she waits on me and I would not want to carry the heavy trays that she carries."

On the other hand, there were always a certain number of men whose work had something of the same problems and they were apt to be less sympathetic. This was particularly true of the farmers in the legislature. There was a good deal of opposition from them because the restaurant owners who were against the bill would say to them, "You work from sun up to sun down. You could not get your work done within eight hours, and it is the same thing with the waitresses."

In spite of all these difficulties, however, eventually the law was passed in 1937 and now the waitresses in Illinois work an eight-hour day within an over-all ten-hour period.

The work for legislation went on and on, year after year. We got a ten-hour-day law in 1909, but it was not until 1937 that the Illinois legislature fell in step with the times and passed an eight-hour law for women. By that time similar laws had been passed in twenty other states and the District of Columbia, and the federal Wage and Hour Law established a standard of minimum wages and maximum hours for both men and women throughout the country in 1938.

In the early days when we worked for hour laws for women, we did so because it seemed to be the only way we could remedy a very bad situation for thousands of women. Regulation of women's hours of work had been declared constitutional because of the effect on their health of long hours and overfatigue. The men did not want to be included in these laws because they felt that through trade union organization they were strong enough to get their own hour regulations and they did not want to have their so-called freedom of contract limited.

Later on, when I was director of the Women's Bureau in the United States Department of Labor, we found after an investigation that when hours of work were limited by law for women, thousands of men too profited by this limitation because if it was necessary for a factory to have a shorter workweek for women, it was often found easier to set one standard for all employees rather than have different hours for men and for women. Now, with the federal Fair Labor Standards Act, the general standard is less than eight hours a day and a forty-hour week for everyone.

It has taken a long time for these standards to be generally accepted, but it has been my experience that each advance in labor legislation has not been especially revolutionary. Instead it has usually been a reflection of standard practice in the better run industries and became a public policy because it was needed chiefly to bring the employers with low standards into line.

Our own work for legislation went hand in hand with our organizing campaigns. After the ten-hour-day law was passed we knew it would never be really effective unless the workers knew about it, so we went to work distributing leaflets telling about the law and how to make complaints if it was not being complied with.

We kept thousands of these leaflets, in five languages, in the storeroom in back of our office on the fourth floor of an old building on La Salle Street near Van Buren. The Chicago Federation of Labor had offices near us on the same floor.

On the way to work one very cold morning, I bought a paper that carried a big story saying that our building had burned down during the night. I went right to the spot to see what had happened and I will never forget the sight that greeted me. All I could see was leaflets lying everywhere and each leaflet said, "Obey, obey, obey" in five different languages. I could also see the corner of our office four flights up and there sat the safe that I had locked before I left the night before and that had all our papers in it. In a day or so when the fire had stopped burning and we knew the walls would not crumble someone went up and got our things out of the safe. But the leaflets were gone forever and I cannot say I was sorry, because I had spent so many Sunday mornings passing them out. I was really glad to see the last of them.

After the fire we moved to better offices at 166 Washington Street, in the same building as the Chicago Federation of Labor, but sometimes we used to get homesick for the old office where we had had so much fun and done so many interesting things. I will always remember one experience we had in the old office before the fire. A friend had given us dozens of bottles of grape juice which she had made during the summer. We kept the bottles in the storeroom, planning to sell them to get money for the league. But the juice fermented, the bottles started popping, and we had grape juice all over the place. Earlier Agnes Johnson had got a shower bath when she bought a couple of bottles, put them in a basket, and then the corks blew out and covered her white shirtwaist with the purple juice.

9

New Channels of Work

IN the summer of 1912 when I was thirty-nine years old I had my first real vacation. Of course, there had been plenty of times before when I was not actually working because I had lost my job or was changing to a new one. Every year, too, I had left work for a week or so to attend the Boot and Shoe Workers executive board meetings and I had been to other labor and Women's Trade Union League conventions. But attending a convention is no vacation.

Agnes Nestor had been in Philadelphia helping with a garment workers' strike. When she got back to Chicago in the middle of the summer, she was very tired and needed a rest. Mrs. Dauchy, who was one of the allies of the Trade Union League and was always helping us in every way, invited Agnes to go to Colorado for a vacation with her sister-in-law, Beatrix Dauchy. Their plans were all made when a few days later at a meeting in the league office, Beatrix came to me and said that Mrs. Dauchy wanted me to go along and have a vacation with her and Agnes. Of course I accepted. Mrs. Dauchy paid all the expenses of our trip and also arranged for us to be outfitted with the clothes we would need. We went to Estes Park. It was a wonderful experience. I had never seen the mountains before and when we arrived late in the afternoon and shot up into the mountains on a big steam sight-seeing

conveyance I held on so hard to my outside seat high up in
the air that I was stiff and sore the next day.

We stayed in the town of Estes for a few days and then
went to a ranch for three weeks and to Long's Peak Inn for
one week. To me, every minute of it was wonderful. I found
that I had not forgotten how to handle horses and although
trail riding was not much like the riding I had done as a child,
the horses were the same and I liked them as much as ever.
We had a good deal of fun together and it was hard to leave
and go back to the work and worries of life in Chicago. The
next year Mrs. Dauchy gave us another trip — a fifteen-day
horseback ride in Yellowstone Park.

From these two experiences I got a real taste for the mountains and for the life in that part of the world, but it was to
be a very long time before I would have a chance to see it
again.

In the meantime, life in Chicago went on with many different kinds of activities, all of them aimed at helping working women. The Chicago Women's Trade Union League had
many irons in the fire and we all found plenty to do. Of
course, my main job was organizing, but that was only part
of the picture and I had many other things to do.

One of my jobs was to help with the work of the Union
Label League. All during the time that I was with the Wom-
en's Trade Union League in Chicago I was a delegate to the
Union Label League and attended all its meetings. This league
was a branch of the Chicago Federation of Labor devoted
entirely to advertising and promoting the use of the union
label on all kinds of commodities.

At one time we were able to do quite a bit with the stores
in getting them to sell union-labeled goods. The allied members of the Women's Trade Union League and many others
helped. We tried to create a customers' demand for the union
label and then we would persuade stores to stock union-made
goods. We had more success with the shoe labels than with

other things because there were many shoe manufacturers working under contract with the union at that time. We were quite successful with the necktiemakers, too, and we had some success with the shirtmakers, but not much. We got the waiters and waitresses to wear their union buttons, and everywhere we urged the use of the union labels. I think the movement has accomplished a good deal, especially among union members, who appreciate what the label means and do not want to buy things that have not been made under decent conditions.

Another interesting committee that I served on while I was with the Chicago Women's Trade Union League was a committee on fire prevention. We knew that there were great fire hazards in most places of employment and we felt that something should be done about them. We would get the information about conditions from the girls who came to our meetings and then we would ask the state department of labor to go in and investigate. Conditions were really bad. Often there were no fire escapes and no exit signs, and almost never were there any fire drills. After we had gotten our facts we would go to the city council, point out the hazards, and try to make the council adopt better fire safety codes. We made some progress, but it really took a couple of big fires and a great many unnecessary deaths before anything like adequate fire protection was established.

One of the Women's Trade Union League activities that I really enjoyed was singing in its chorus. Chicago had developed small parks in congested areas where the children and older people could hold festivals. In those areas, most of the people were immigrants and the problem was to give them an outlet for the expression of their old country's culture. The league started the custom of having a series of festivals at which the songs of the countries the immigrants came from were sung. I was not much of a singer, but I liked music and took part in these festivals with much pleasure. We had to practice a good deal, singing Polish, Italian, German, and Irish songs. I remember we rebelled one time because our teacher was always making us sing lullabies, and we wanted something livelier. These festivals were so successful that they were finally taken over by the city.

Another project that was also eventually taken over by the city was our health committee. Many of the girls who came to our meetings and whom we met in other ways had very serious health problems. But because they had so little money and also because they did not know whom to go to, they did nothing about it. If they had bad coughs, or anything else the matter with them, they would dose themselves with some medicine that a friend had told them about, when they could afford to buy it, and struggle along hoping that they would get better. Of course, sometimes they did get better, but there were many cases of serious and permanent illness that we knew could have been avoided or helped if they had had some kind of medical attention in time. So we started a health program for them. We were able to get the cooperation of a number of women doctors and we persuaded the girls to go to them for examinations and treatment if necessary. We kept up this work for several years until it was finally taken over by the city health clinics.

Then we started an immigration committee, which in the end was taken over by a committee organized under the state government with Grace Abbott in charge. Through this committee we called attention to the plight of the immigrants coming into the city. We had people meet them at the station and help them orient themselves. Whenever they were going on farther west, we helped them to change trains. Grace Abbott did much of that work; Sophonisba Breckinridge and other faculty members of the University of Chicago and their students also helped. I was on the committee, as a member of the league, for a number of years.

Perhaps the most important, and certainly the most interesting, of the many committees I served on while I was with the national league was the one that set up and directed training courses for organizers. For a while I was chairman of that committee and had charge of the program. Our purpose was to get the young women who were working in a trade to take a leading part in the trade union movement. If they were going to do this we knew they must be equipped through experience and training to play their parts well. For instance, if a girl was going to be secretary or treasurer of her union, she had to know how to keep books and how to prepare minutes. If she was to be a leader she had to know how to conduct meetings, and if she was to be influential in setting policies she had to know also some of the basic facts of economics and history. So, in 1914, the national league started a training school for girls who were selected by their local leagues. Their expenses were paid partly by the local leagues, but mostly by the national league, which raised a special fund for this purpose. The training for each girl lasted from six months to a year. I do not think we ever had more than six or eight students at one time because they were full-time students and the cost kept the number down. But it was well worth the effort we put into it. Aside from training in calling meetings, presiding at meetings, keeping books and minutes, which the girls got from actual experience at meetings we took them to, we were able to get Northwestern University and later on the School of Civics and Philanthropy and the University of Chicago to let the girls attend their classes in economics. In return, the college students in these classes were allowed to attend the Sunday meetings of the Chicago Federation of Labor. We found that our students contributed as much to these university classes as they got out of them, because when they took part in the class discussions they were able to speak from everyday experience and in that way they brought reality to the questions that were only theories for the regular students.

This training school continued until 1926. In the thirteen years of its existence forty-four girls working in seventeen different trades were trained. I think it was one of the most important things that was done for women in the trade union movement. Most of the women who attended the school turned out to be leaders. Even if they were not elected to any position in their unions or leagues, they made themselves felt.

Later on this kind of training for women was taken up by the Bryn Mawr summer school and other workers' education groups, and has been of the greatest service to the working woman everywhere.

It was in the early part of 1917 while I was immersed in all the various activities of the trade union movement and the Women's Trade Union League that I was pushed into a new channel of work, which, although I did not know it at the time, was to end by taking me away from Chicago and into federal work in Washington for the rest of my life. At that time, as organizer for the league, I had been called in to help with a strike of one thousand women making small machine parts at the Stewart and Warner factory in Chicago. One morning after the strike had been going on for a week without seeming to accomplish anything and while I was exceedingly busy working out a program with the strikers in a hall on the outskirts of the city, I received a summons to come immediately to Mrs. Robins' office. I was too busy to leave, so instead she came to see me at ten o'clock in the morning and said, "You will have to take the noon train to Washington today," explaining that I was to attend a meeting of a committee that had been set up by Mr. Gompers, president of the American Federation of Labor, to act in an advisory capacity to him in matters affecting women's interests. "Why," I replied, "I can't possibly go. I can't desert the girls here and now in the midst of their troubles." They knew and trusted me and would feel I was playing them false if I ran away from them at a critical point even on such an important mission as this one in Washington.

My protests were in vain; Mrs. Robins was firm, insisting that I must go and volunteering to take my place with the strikers during my absence. So off I went on what appeared

*Mary Anderson at the time of her appointment as director of the
Women's Bureau, U.S. Department of Labor*

Mary van Kleeck

Agnes Peterson

Leaders in the movement to improve working conditions for women

Mary N. Winslow

Elisabeth Christman

HARRIS & EWING PHOTO

Margaret Bondfield, British minister of labor after World War I

Dr. Anna Howard Shaw, noted suffrage leader

Mary Anderson, center, inspecting a plane factory during World War II

Dr. Herbert Davis, president of Smith College, with Mary Anderson in 1941 when she received an honorary degree from the college

Mary Anderson: "I know that I have had a fine, full life"

to me to be just a war tangent. When I returned to Chicago a little later the strike was over. But I had started on the trail to Washington and soon I was returning there at more or less regular intervals during the early months of the war.

I have often wondered what the course of my life would have been if I had not served on that committee. Here again it was Mrs. Robins and the league that were the deciding factors in starting me in a new line of work. I had not been appointed a member of the committee when it was first set up. In fact, when Mr. Gompers first announced the membership of the committee we discovered that he had not included in it even one trade union woman. I remember that one of the first members to be appointed was Lillian Russell, the actress! When we read in the papers of the women who had been appointed some of us trade union workers sent telegrams to Mr. Gompers protesting against the omission of trade union women. The result was that those who sent telegrams were appointed to the committee and that was the way I got my first assignment to Washington.

Mrs. J. Borden Harriman was chairman of the committee and among the many members was Mary McDowell of Chicago, with whom I had worked for so many years.

We met at the Lafayette Hotel in Washington and discussed questions of women's employment such as what jobs women could take in the war industries and how working conditions for them could be improved. At first, I used to travel from Chicago for the meetings, but finally the league decided it would be better for me to stay in Washington and do some organizing there. I worked with the employees of the Bureau of Engraving and Printing and also as a representative of the Boot and Shoe Workers Union. In the latter capacity I went as a member of a committee of trade unionists to the secretary of war, Newton Baker, to complain that the union firms, especially in the shoe and glove industries, were not getting proper consideration in the letting of war contracts.

As the weeks went on and the meetings of the women's

advisory committee continued, many of us, especially Miss McDowell and I, became very dissatisfied with our progress. We knew that our function was purely advisory, but even so not much seemed to be accomplished. The people who came to the meetings reported on what was going on in the states and there was a rather vague attempt to recommend standards, but mostly the meetings were just an exchange of information, some of it pertinent and some of it not.

Coming in on the train from Chicago one day, Miss McDowell and I developed what we thought would be a good plan for the work of the committee. We decided that when the meeting started and the members were all there I was to try to get their signatures to this plan and then present it as a kind of referendum.

During the meeting while I was trying to get signatures, a young woman came in and sat down beside me. She was a very crisp, intelligent-looking person, and although I did not know who she was, I felt instinctively that she would have a clear-headed approach to the work we were trying to do. I handed her the memorandum and she looked it over and signed it. When I saw the signature I found that she was Mary van Kleeck from the Russell Sage Foundation. This was the beginning of our long association, first in the Ordnance Department of the War Department and later in the Woman in Industry Service of the Department of Labor.

Miss van Kleeck was making a study of the feasibility of employing women in the ordnance storage plants at the request of Dean Herman Schneider of the University of Cincinnati, who had been appointed to head the Labor Division in the Ordnance Department. I saw her again in Buffalo where the American Federation of Labor had its convention in the fall of 1917 and where I was a delegate for the Boot and Shoe Workers Union. She showed me her report and we discussed it together, but I did not see her again until the beginning of 1918 when I came to Washington for another of the advisory committee meetings. Then we had lunch together and she told me that she had been asked by Dean Schneider to organize a women's division in the Ordnance Department and to head that division. She said she wanted a labor woman with her in this work and that she had talked with many people, who all said to get Mary Anderson. I told her that I was interested in the idea but that I could not decide at that time. When I got back to Chicago I talked it over with Mrs. Robins and the others in the league and they said that if I wanted to do it, I should take a leave of absence. I took three months' leave of absence from the league and came to Washington, where I have spent the rest of my life.

10

Women in Ordnance

IT was in January 1918 that I first started to work for the government of the United States. As it turned out, the federal government was my employer for the next twenty-five years, but I did not think when I first began that I had a permanent career in government ahead of me. In fact, after I had been there only a few weeks, I felt that my job was futile, that there was nothing particularly for me to do, and I decided that when my three months were up I would go back to the league.

Before she took over the Women's Division of the Ordnance Department Mary van Kleeck had recommended to General William Crozier, chief of ordnance, certain standards for the employment of women that should be followed in the ordnance plants where women were working. These standards were incorporated in General Orders Number 13, issued by General Crozier and by the quartermaster general. It was our job to work with the ordnance plants to get these standards put into effect and to help with the various problems that came up when women were being employed.

The enunciation of the standards was very important and paved the way for the program of the Woman in Industry Service when it was started a few months later. Before I joined the division Miss van Kleeck had already succeeded in placing

women personnel directors in every arsenal. But on the whole
I do not think that we accomplished as much as we should
have, chiefly because there was a great deal of antagonism to
us in the division. Dean Schneider was an excellent chief, but
the men he had to depend on did not like us to be in on the
ground floor. Many of the men appointed had been employment managers in stores or connected with industry in some
other way. They were put into uniforms and felt that they
had to run the show. As usual, they did not want women to
interfere in any way.

Women had not, before that time, taken any part in the
work of the War Department. We were a new phenomenon
and they were distrustful of us. I think they thought of me
particularly as what they probably called a "red-eyed labor
leader" who would be destructive rather than helpful. The
men's attitude was due to both ignorance and prejudice, but
I think they were honestly of the opinion that we would
disturb things rather than do what we wanted to, which was
help in creating the standards that would give the best production.

As a result of this attitude and probably, too, because I was
so new to this kind of work I felt that I was very much submerged and that there was little chance to really implement
any standards for women. The same thing was true in the
different cities and states where ordnance divisions were organized under the army. We had the greatest difficulty getting
into a plant to find out what was going on.

I remember going to Bridgeport with a group of several
men and one other woman to inspect some factories and see
that production was facilitated by proper working conditions.
The group never got into a factory. We waited for the head
of our expedition to tell us when we could go into a factory
to see what the conditions were. Day after day he put us off
saying the management was "about" ready to let us in. After
nearly a week of waiting we left in disgust.

Another time, Mary van Kleeck and I stopped in Pitts-

burgh for one day to see conditions in some of the many ordnance plants there. We were met by an officer from the
Ordnance Department the minute we got to the hotel, were
taken to the office, taken to lunch, taken through one plant
in the afternoon, taken to dinner that night. We were so
closely chaperoned that until we took the train that night
we could not so much as say "hello" to one another. Naturally, we did not find out much about the conditions of wom-
en's employment.

After a few such experiences, I was about ready to pack
up and go back to Chicago, but on my return to Washington from one of these inspection trips in the spring of 1918,
I got a telephone call from Felix Frankfurter. He was then
acting with the secretary of labor planning the organization
of divisions in the Department of Labor that had been recommended by the Committee on National Defense. Mr. Frankfurter told me that they were going to set up a woman in
industry division in the department just as soon as appropriations were authorized by Congress. He hinted that I might
like to come into that division. He did not ask me directly,
but said that the secretary of labor had mentioned it and
wanted to find out if I would be willing to come. I said I
might be interested and then Mr. Frankfurter asked me to
lunch at the "House of Truth," which was what everyone
called the house on Nineteenth Street where he and a number
of other men lived. There were six or seven men there at
lunch and it was quite an ordeal for me because I felt that
they were looking me over and I found it rather embarrassing.

They must have made a favorable report because the next
day the secretary of labor called me and I went over to see
him. When I got to his office, he said, "I want to move you
and Miss van Kleeck over here to take charge of the Woman
in Industry Service. I don't know which of you ought to be
the director and which the assistant, but you can settle that
between you."

I replied that I thought Miss van Kleeck ought to be the

director as she knew more about how to organize this kind of work than I did. He said, "All right, I'm going to make the appointments in a very few days."

As soon as our interview was over, I went straight to the telegraph office and sent a very guarded telegram to Mary van Kleeck, who was out in the field, telling her to come home, which she did the next day. We then went to see the secretary and told him we would do the job. Finally, the appropriation came through and the appointments were made in the latter part of June 1918.

The establishment of the Woman in Industry Service in the Department of Labor was the culmination of many years of work and agitation on the part of women and women's organizations, especially the National Women's Trade Union League. Mary McDowell and Jane Addams had been among the first to get interested in having some division of the federal government to look after the interests of women in industry and they had sold that idea to a good many other people. In 1906 they had gone to Washington to see President Theodore Roosevelt and persuaded him that the government should make an investigation of the conditions of employment of women and children. The President was cordial and told them that anything the women wanted they were going to get. When it came to granting suffrage to women, it took him some time to come around to this point of view, but apparently it did not need so much persuading to get his support for an investigation. In 1907 Congress voted an appropriation and the great study of women and child wage earners was made. The report of this investigation was the most important and far-reaching statement of the conditions under which women and children were employed that has ever been made. For many years it was used as the basis for programs to improve conditions, and it furnished source material for every group that was interested in industrial problems.

The result of this report was the establishment of the Women's Division of the Bureau of Labor Statistics in the Depart-

ment of Commerce and Labor. This division was directed by
Marie Obenauer, but it did not survive very long.

Then began the agitation for a women's bureau in the
newly created Department of Labor. The National Women's
Trade Union League was the first of the national organizations to pass a resolution for such a bureau at its convention
in 1909.

After this resolution had been passed we tried to get support for it from the American Federation of Labor. The federation, so far as the officers were concerned, was with us, but
did nothing about it for a number of years. In 1916 at the
American Federation of Labor convention in Baltimore, to
which I was a delegate from the National Women's Trade
Union League and Elisabeth Christman a delegate from the
glove workers' union, we put in a resolution asking support
for a women's bureau in the Department of Labor.

We asked for a hearing before the resolutions committee,
but were put off from day to day. Finally, we heard that the
committee was going to report on the resolutions, and I went
to the committee and asked when we would have a hearing.
They still said they would let us know.

The next thing to happen was that the committee reported
there was no support given to this resolution. I was stunned
and there was no time to do anything. Mr. Gompers, who was
with us, asked for a hearing and appeared before the resolutions committee, but they still did not change their attitude.
Their excuse was that the bureau would be created just to
make a position for a "silk-stockinged" woman. The garment
workers, who were very strong on the resolutions committee,
were the ones that opposed it, because of the old score against
Mrs. Robins at the time of the United Garment Workers'
strike in Chicago.

The next morning, when the convention convened, I asked
for the floor. Gompers knew what I was going to do, and, to
give me a chance to get forward through the crowd, he
walked up and down the platform for several minutes while

I came up. Then he motioned and I made my speech, saying
that I did not know who was going to be appointed if such
a bureau was formed, but, after all, we could trust the secretary of labor to see that the right person was selected and that
whoever was appointed, the establishment of a women's bureau would be a great achievement. But nothing happened;
the delegates did not change their attitude; and the Woman
in Industry Service was eventually established, without the
official support of the American Federation of Labor, because
it was a necessity of the war.

Clara Tead took over the Women's Division in the Ordnance Department, and on July 9, 1918, Mary van Kleeck
and I moved to the Department of Labor.

11

The Woman in Industry Service

WHEN the Woman in Industry Service was started we did not have much of a setup. At first there were just Miss van Kleeck and a secretary and I. After a few weeks I was able to get a secretary, too, and gradually we built up a small staff. When we got going, most of us slept in a Pullman upper berth during the night and worked during the day, visiting factories and making suggestions to the women's employers for standard conditions of sanitation, hours of work, and safety, because the factories at that time were very lax in all these matters.

We had a very hectic feeling in the first days of organizing the service. We knew it was important to get started immediately because nothing had been done about women during the first part of the war. They were going into war plants in great numbers and working under very bad conditions. They did grinding and assembling, worked in the TNT factories, loaded shells, and did all kinds of other work for heavy machinery and guns. They were doing good work, but they did not get much recognition, and because there were no statistics, no one knew how many were employed. I think, really, until the Woman in Industry Service got started, women were the "forgotten men" of that time.

My first job with the service was typical of the kind of

problems we ran into. When the service was officially established, I was attending a meeting of the national executive board of the Boot and Shoe Workers Union in Boston. I resigned from the board at that meeting and got back to Washington a week after the service was created. As soon as I arrived, Mary van Kleeck called me to say there was a meeting at ten o'clock that she wanted me to attend. The meeting was to consider a request from the Manufacturers' Association of Niagara Falls to employ women at night in the chemical plants there. I was asked to go on a midnight train to New York and appear before the New York department of labor, of which John Mitchell was then commissioner, to ask that Nelle Swartz, who was head of the bureau of women and children in New York, go with me to Niagara Falls to investigate the situation.

Our request was granted and Nelle and I went to Niagara Falls and called upon the secretary of the Manufacturers' Association. He said they wanted women to work loading and wheeling wheelbarrows full of sulphur. It was the first time I had heard that there were chemical factories at Niagara Falls. I had always thought of the Falls as a great wonder of the world. I had heard about them before I came to America, and it was a great shock to me to find that these factories with such terrible working conditions were there. Even the trees around the factories were stripped of leaves by the chemical fumes. The workers' houses were among these bare trees. It was not only the workers themselves who had to live in this devastation, but their families and the rest of the community.

We went from one factory to another all day and then we came back to Washington and made our report to Miss van Kleeck, telling her of the very bad conditions we found in almost all the plants. She then got in touch with the Public Health Service and she and some of the doctors went to Niagara Falls to investigate the situation further. Besides the chemical plants, there were carborundum factories where the conditions were very bad because the work created a metallic dust and there were no exhausts. The dust was so thick you could hardly see the worker at the next machine. Then there was a plant manufacturing storage batteries that wanted to employ more women. This was a very perilous occupation for women because the effects of lead poisoning are especially serious for them, causing sterility, miscarriages, and death of babies during the first year of their lives.

Although the armistice came before our investigations and recommendations were completed and there was no longer a need for increased employment of women in these plants, our experience there had taught us that the important thing for us to do was not so much to regulate *women's* employment as to regulate instead the *conditions* of employment for all workers. Except for the lead industries where there was a special danger to women that they should never be exposed to, we found that conditions of employment could usually be arranged so that women could be efficiently employed. There is no reason in the world why women should not handle wheelbarrows if the load is not too heavy and the woman is taught how to wheel it properly. The same is true of loading and other weight-carrying. The important thing is to remember that women should not be employed in any industry, or men either, until the work is made *safe*. It is the conditions that should be regulated and not the person.

When the secretary of labor announced the organization of the Woman in Industry Service and our appointments, he made a very good statement about what we were to do which I think is worth quoting here.

In recognition of the great importance to the nation of the work of women in industry, and the urgent necessity for a national policy in determining the conditions of their employment, I have urged and Congress has now granted the necessary authority to establish a Women's Division in the Department of Labor. Its immediate task will be to develop in the industries of the country policies and methods which will result in the most effective use of women's services in production for the war, while at the same time preventing their employment under injurious conditions. Its large and very necessary aim will be to focus attention on the national importance of the conditions of women's work as influencing industrial standards and as affecting the welfare of the entire nation.

The Women's Division will be charged primarily with determining policies rather than carrying on detailed administration. Because of this policy-making function of the Women's Division, its director will serve as a member of the War Labor Policies Board. It will coordinate work for women in other divisions of the Department of Labor, working with and through them, in order to bring about united action by the States in national problems of women's work. The Women's Division will concern itself primarily with war conditions, but will be mindful of the need for observing and interpreting the tendencies in women's employment which are likely to have permanent social effects.

The Women's Division has been established in response to needs widely felt by all, men as well as women, who are conscious of the increasing share women must have in the industrial activities of the war. The problems of women in industry are so manifold and complex that a clearing house of thought and leadership is needed in the National Government. The Women's Division has been established to give this leadership.

Since we had an appropriation of only thirty thousand dollars for this work, it is obvious that we had to spread ourselves rather thin to cover it all.

I think our most important job was issuing the standards for the employment of women. It was the first time the federal government had taken a practical stand on conditions of employment for women, and although the standards were only recommendations and had no legal force, they were a very important statement of policy and were widely used in all parts of the country.

As a code for the employment of women these standards have stood throughout the years. They are just about as good today as they were the day they were issued, except that the hours now are shorter. The standards set at that time were these: an eight-hour day and a forty-eight-hour week; Saturday half-holiday; one day of rest in seven; three quarters of an hour for a meal; rest periods; no night work; equal pay for men and women; a minimum wage rate to cover the cost of living for dependents and not merely for the individual; safe and sanitary working conditions; prohibition of women's employment in occupations especially hazardous to them, such as certain processes in the lead industries; prohibition of industrial homework; participation of workers in enforcement of standards and establishing good working conditions; establishment of personnel departments and appointment of women to supervisory positions.

When they were finally issued, the standards were not very different from those of General Orders Number 13, which had been issued by the chief of ordnance, but we had to work hard with all kinds of groups, in the government and out of it, before we could get their endorsement and could decide on the final form. Our first step was to draw up a tentative draft of the standards and submit it to various interested persons and agencies because we knew that being only recommendations, the standards would have no real effect unless they had the united support of everyone interested.

Immediately after the service was organized, we set up a Council on Women in Industry composed of representatives of every division of the Department of Labor and other federal departments having work related to problems of women in industry. Its membership included the Women's Division of the Ordnance Department, the Women's Section of the Railroad Administration, the Federal Board for Vocational Education, the Committee on Women in Industry of the Advisory Commission, the Woman's Committee of the Council of National Defense, and, from the Department of Labor, representatives of the services concerned with investigation and inspection, training and dilution, information and education, working conditions, the United States Employment Service, the Immigration Bureau, the Children's Bureau, the

Bureau of Naturalization, the Bureau of Labor Statistics, the United States Housing Corporation, the War Labor Board, and the War Labor Policies Board.

It was a large group and we met frequently, sometimes as often as once a week. Among the members I remember especially were Dr. C. E. A. Winslow, the noted public health authority, Clara Tead of the Women's Division of the Ordnance Department, and Pauline Goldmark of the Women's Section of the Railroad Administration. Felix Frankfurter represented the War Labor Policies Board. Mrs. J. Borden Harriman came for the Committee on Women in Industry of the American Federation of Labor Advisory Commission. Julia Lathrop represented the Children's Bureau of the United States Department of Labor, and Ethelbert Stewart the Bureau of Labor Statistics, of which he later became chief. This council was a forum for discussion of the various problems that came before the Woman in Industry Service, and it was very helpful in getting an over-all picture of what was going on and as an agency through which we could publicize our standards and recommendations.

In addition to the council we had a special committee on the standards with representatives of the War Department, the Navy Department, the Public Health Service, the Working Conditions Service in the Department of Labor, and others. This committee met frequently because Miss van Kleeck was anxious to get out the standards as quickly as possible.

We submitted the standards to all kinds of people — to the council and then to a great many employers, to the labor commissioners of the States, to labor unions, to women's organizations, and to as many of the people as we could reach through publicity.

There was a great deal of discussion of them, especially by the Public Health Service, which was not particularly in favor of the eight-hour day.

It took longer than it should have to get the standards issued because the men on the committee could not agree and there were some delaying tactics because they were afraid the standards would interfere with the production of war materials. The result was that they were not issued until after the war. Most of the delaying tactics, I think, came from the War Department. Its officials seemed to be agreed that the standards should be issued, but they were so afraid of any disturbance in war production that they put it off time after time. Also, in the War Department it took a long time to get the endorsement of the divisions that had to do with standards before they went up for final approval.

There was a tremendous difference of opinion at the meetings of the committee to consider the standards. The members went over them and over them. Many meetings were just arguments. On the whole the members agreed, but objected to little words here and there; sometimes it was only a punctuation mark, but it had to be changed. It was generally understood that these standards were suggestions only, with no legal force back of them. But we felt that if they were issued as suggestions, many employers would put them into effect.

Finally, after what seemed to us an interminable delay, we submitted the standards to the secretary of labor and the War Labor Policies Board on October 18, 1918. They were adopted by the board immediately, but were modified on October 25, because it seemed likely that the armistice would be signed soon. Then came the armistice and the standards had to be changed again, this time to meet peace conditions. They were finally issued on December 12, 1918, as the basis for a program of reconstruction.

In the years that followed, literally hundreds of thousands of copies of the standards were circulated throughout the country. They were publicized through exhibits made by the Woman in Industry Service and later by the Women's Bureau. We showed them in charts, in photographs, in motion pictures, and in posters. We wrote popular stories about them for the use of women's clubs and other groups. We made investigations to support them. In fact, for many years much of the program of the Woman in Industry Service and the Women's Bureau was based on them. They were accepted as a goal by almost every group working to improve conditions for women. They were incorporated to a great extent in legislation, and they were adopted by many employers voluntarily. They were indeed the most important thing the Woman in Industry did and their influence on working conditions for women cannot be overemphasized.

12

Women Workers in World War I

ONE of the jobs in the early days of the Woman in Industry Service that I got a thrill out of was attending the meetings of the War Labor Policies Board. The chairman of this board was Felix Frankfurter, and the person representing the Navy Department was the assistant secretary of the navy, Franklin D. Roosevelt. The director of the Woman in Industry Service was a member of this board and when she was out of town I took her place. Our chief responsibility on this board was to advise how women could be employed most effectively in the munitions factories and in the heavy industries. Increased production was necessary and, with the labor shortage, a greater use of women seemed to be the only answer.

We had a good many tussles with the board on matters of policy. I think the most serious one occurred when the board wanted us to set up a list of industries in which women should be employed. We felt we could not do that because, if they were really needed, women could work almost anywhere, provided the working conditions were satisfactory.

I will never forget a meeting we had with Mr. Frankfurter to discuss this subject. It was a warm spring day and we met in the park near the Washington Monument. Mary van Kleeck and I sat on a bench and Mr. Frankfurter sat on the grass at our feet while we had a hot discussion, trying to make him come over to our point of view. Nowadays, when I hear of Mr. Baruch and his park-bench office, I often think of that meeting and how Mr. Frankfurter was ahead of Mr. Baruch, not only by meeting in the park first, but by comfortably sitting on the grass instead of using the rather stiff bench, which he left for Mary and me.

It took a good deal of persuading to bring him around. At one time he even suggested that if we would not issue such a list of occupations for women he would see that the matter was taken out of our hands and the list issued by some other agency. But we stuck to our guns and in the end we won out with the decision that instead of offering a list of occupations in which women should be substituted for men, we would promulgate standards with the statement that in any occupation in which these standards were upheld increased employment of women would be desirable.

Another thing we had to watch out for was the substitution of women for men at very much lower wages than the men had been getting. One of these cases arose in Buffalo where a firm manufacturing hand grenades applied for permission to employ women at night. The War Department was very anxious to get greater production of hand grenades and was insisting that women be employed. The firm had appealed to the state department of labor for permission to employ women at night, but had been turned down. Then the matter landed in our lap, and I went to Buffalo to investigate.

When I came into Buffalo there was a streetcar strike on. I called up the firm, which was located just a little bit out of town, and the superintendent had to drive in and fetch me because there was no other way to get there. On the way he told me how wonderful the women were and what good jobs they did. He said he wanted to employ them at night because the men were so inefficient that what they produced was only fit for the scrap heap.

I asked about the pay and he said, "The men get forty cents an hour with a fifteen per cent bonus, and we are starting the women at twenty-five cents an hour." I asked why they would pay so much more to these inefficient men. His answer was that the women had no family responsibilities. Then I said, "Do you really know that? And what family responsibilities have the men?" He replied that he really could not tell what responsibilities the men had, and he admitted that he had a widow with three children working for him. After that, I asked him the real reason for paying women less than men and he said, "If I paid them the same there would be a revolution. There is a tacit understanding that women should not make over twenty-five cents an hour."

I came back to Washington and made my report, but since the armistice was signed the following week, we never had to decide this case, which combined two of the most difficult problems we had to deal with — unequal pay and night work for women.

In the standards we had said that wages should be set by the job and not by the sex of the worker, but we did not get very far in having this standard accepted. We tried to push it but ran up against a good deal of opposition from employers, and even from labor in general. The men always felt they were inferior if they did not get higher wages than women and they never seemed to realize the danger to their own wage rates if women were permitted to work at the same jobs for less pay. Then there was the difficulty of finding out whether or not jobs were really the same for men and women. Some slight adjustment in machinery or difference in working conditions might make it seem that there was a real difference in the job. Of course, the employers took advantage of this and it really was necessary to have a job analysis to clear up the conditions of each job. Added to this, there was no enforcement machinery. The result was that we did not make much progress on "equal pay" until years later during World War II.

The regulation of night work for women was a real headache for us in the Woman in Industry Service. At that time twelve states had laws prohibiting the employment of women and girls during the night hours. It was generally recognized that night work, especially for women, was inefficient, a menace to health and to the welfare of the family. But in their drive to increase production, the War and Navy departments, as well as the employers, put great pressure on us to permit night work for women. We were in something of a quandary. Of course, we wanted as much as anyone else to increase war production, but we did not think that a wholesale abolition of legal safeguards was the way to do it.

We took the matter up with everyone we could think of in trying to work out a satisfactory solution. We called a conference of organizations concerned with standards of working conditions for women — the Council on Women in Industry, the National Consumers League, the National Women's Trade Union League, the American Association for Labor Legislation, the trade unions, state industrial commissions and departments of labor. Then we called a special conference of trade union women and, besides that, we got special advice from the War Industries Board and from representatives of employers. The policy finally worked out was that exemptions for employment of women at night would be issued for a limited period only after investigation of each specific request and decision that an emergency existed. But here again the armistice came before final action was taken and it was not until the next war that we had the same problem on our hands and worked out practically the same solution too.

Shortly before and after the armistice, the Woman in Industry Service began receiving many complaints about the treatment of women in factories that were under federal control. We passed these complaints on to the War Department, and they came back and asked us to make an investigation. I remember talking this matter over with Walter Lippmann, who was at that time an assistant to the secretary of war.

The chief complaints were from the clothing industry, where the women were working a ten-hour day at very low wages and with poor working conditions, and from some tobacco plants. Discovery of the conditions in the tobacco rehandling plants led us to start a general study of the employment of Negro women in industry, hoping that if we found out the real facts something would be done to improve their conditions. We did not get very far with this because we had no authority to enforce our recommendations and the employers did not take our suggestions seriously. They apparently felt that as long as they could get Negro women to work under such conditions there was no incentive to clean things up. However, we did find out under what terrible conditions and discriminations Negro women were sometimes employed and later on we got a very fine Negro woman on our staff who went to the same plants and made a reinvestigation. She turned in a good report and we found that there had been a good deal of mopping up since our first visits.

The question of the substitution of women for men in various occupations was one that we had to watch very closely. If the jobs were desirable there was usually a good deal of opposition to women's employment by the men in the industry, but if the jobs were low grade and no one else wanted them, there was much enthusiasm about women taking them over.

One of the most hotly contested cases was that of the women streetcar conductors in Cleveland. Women had been put on the Cleveland streetcars as conductors and ticket punchers and the union objected, saying that the work was dangerous and that there were plenty of men available. They wanted to disqualify the women and get a ruling from the War Labor Board saying that women could not be employed. Rose Moriarity appeared before the board for the women, and also Dr. Anna Howard Shaw, the great suffrage leader, who was at that time the head of the Women's Division of the Council of National Defense. As a result of the arguments presented, the War Labor Board decided that it was perfectly feasible to employ women and that the company had a right to employ them if it wanted to.

I think the decision of the board must have been influenced by the eloquent appeal made by Dr. Shaw, who was one of the finest speakers I have ever heard. Her speech in this case was so important that we had a section of it reprinted on a small card that I have kept with me always. It is worth quoting here because it is such a fine expression of what all of us who are working women feel about our rights to a job of our own choosing.

The time has come when it is neither the right of men, nor the duty of men, nor justice for men to decide problems of work for women.

When the service of the worker and of the world shall be opened to the world workers then let us be tested by our ability to be faithful in that service. If we fail then let us fail, but do not let us fail by the direction of men or by the direction of any group of people.

And therefore I claim that the time has come now when we women have a right to ask that we shall be free to labor where our labor is needed, that we shall be free to serve in the capacity for which we are fitted. No human being can tell what another human being can do until that human being has had the opportunity to test himself. And so it has been with women.

13

The Women's Bureau Is Established

WHEN I first came to Washington with the Woman in Industry Service, the living conditions were just about as bad as they were twenty-five years later during World War II. I had to move many times. The frequent changes and uncomfortable quarters did not make my work any easier. At first I shared a room with another woman on Columbia Road. It was a very small room and when the summer came it was so hot I could not bear it. Then I had a piece of luck when Mrs. Gifford Pinchot turned over to Elisabeth Christman and me for the summer her lovely home on Rhode Island Avenue. We got eighteen girls to live with us and we all ran the house together. It was a lot of fun and much more comfortable than any other place we could get.

In the fall, when Mrs. Pinchot rented the house, Elisabeth and I could not find an apartment anywhere, so we finally settled in a little room in a hotel down by the Capitol. We paid regular hotel rates for this room, two and a half dollars a day, but it was not worth it. The room had two cots, but it was so small there was not space enough for both of us to dress at the same time. We had no closet and our clothes had to hang on pegs all around the room. We had to share the bathroom with several other people. Altogether, it was very uncomfortable but we stuck it out there until Miss May Ladenburg, a society girl from New York, fixed up a little house on M Street off Connecticut Avenue. She got priorities for work on this house because she was going to have war workers in it. Elisabeth and I were the war workers. We finally moved in on the top floor where we had a little sitting room, bedroom, and bath. We were able to get some of our meals there and it was very nice. Elisabeth finally moved back to Chicago after the war was over, but I stayed on alone for quite a while until Miss Ladenburg moved back to New York and I was out of a home again.

Then I got a small room in a hotel on H Street. There, too, I paid almost hotel prices. It had a dining room with fairly good food, which was helpful. My room was on the top floor and had a telephone on the wall and a bed with slats which fell down almost every night. One of the cane chairs in the room was tied together with rope. It was claimed that Lafayette had stayed at this hotel and we said, "Well, the Lafayette furniture is still there!"

After some months, Julia Lathrop, chief of the Children's Bureau, went to Europe for about three months and let me have her apartment while she was away. I then lived in luxury at the Ontario, looking over Rock Creek Park. It was a lovely apartment. However, every morning about four o'clock all the animals in the zoo started to make their routine noises. First, the lions, tigers, and owls had their evening solos before they went to bed. They woke up the day animals who started in too. I got used to it and the noise did not bother me after a while. When Miss Lathrop returned I went back to the hotel on H Street.

There was not much comfort or luxury for any of us government workers during these days in Washington, but we did not mind it. We were so busy it did not make a great deal of difference what kind of home life we had, so long as we had a bed to sleep on, because we never had time for home life anyway. We worked all day and in the evenings too, and about half the time we were traveling about the country, sleeping on the train at night and inspecting factories and consulting with officials during the day.

It was a hard life, but it was exciting and it did not bother us so long as we felt we were accomplishing something.

After the service had been operating for a few months we began to accumulate a larger staff. Anne Larrabee was the first person to join us. She was Miss van Kleeck's secretary, and has given years of devoted and intelligent service to the Women's Bureau ever since — as my secretary, then as chief clerk, and finally as administrative assistant to the present director.

Then we got Agnes Peterson from the department of labor in Minnesota to take charge of our contacts with state labor departments. She was well known not only in her own state but throughout the country. She had great enthusiasm and was full of vitality and ideas. Sometimes they carried her a little too far, but her strong political sense and her wide contacts proved of great value to the bureau. Agnes eventually became assistant director of the Women's Bureau and stayed on for many years until she had to retire because of ill health.

To head our field investigations we got May Allinson, who was an experienced and capable investigator. Her tragic death while directing an investigation in Indiana in December 1918 was a great loss to us and to the women in industry for whom she literally gave her life.

Our chief clerk was Lillian Lewis, who was invaluable to us because she had been chief clerk of the Children's Bureau and knew all the government regulations thoroughly. Miss Lewis stayed with the bureau until her death and served it well, but she was something of a problem too. She got excited easily and her excitement usually carried over to other members of the staff. Later on, when I was the director of the bureau, I had to learn how to handle her. If I asked her to let me know how much money we had left to finish the fiscal year I would get various answers. Once she said that I would have to call in all our field workers because our money had run out but when I told her to look the records over again she found we had more money than she had thought and the crisis was over. I did not altogether blame her. Government regulations are very complicated and it takes a good deal of experience and patience to unwind the red tape. We generally came out all right in the end and her knowledge of how to get things done was very useful to us.

Among our first investigators we had Caroline Manning and Ethel Best, who stayed on with us for many years and played a major part in the development of the Women's Bureau. Caroline came to us from the Children's Bureau. She too was from Minnesota. A college graduate, she had been for some years an investigator in the Minnesota department of labor. She was a very quiet and determined woman, with a highly developed critical sense when it came to evaluating the situation in an industry or plant. At that time she usually found that she was justified in her adverse opinion of conditions. She developed into a highly skilled investigator and field supervisor.

Ethel Best made a good teammate for Caroline. She was very small and very frail but her spirit was indomitable. She had such a friendly and understanding attitude toward everyone that she got almost complete cooperation from employers and great devotion from the investigators who worked under her direction.

One of our most important activities was the educational campaign we started to stimulate interest in the standards. We set up a pictorial division to provide material for meetings of women's organizations and labor unions, to make a photographic record of the work women did in war industries, and to illustrate good and bad standards of working conditions.

I remember our panel exhibit, which was very amateurish in comparison with what is used now but which was very useful at that time. This first exhibit consisted of panels of gray beaverboard with lettering that we pasted on ourselves because we did not have enough money to have the lettering done and there was no one in the office who could do it. We got little black letters with mucilage on the back and made our own captions from them. This was done during the hottest part of one of the hottest summers in Washington. While we were working on these panels we could not turn on a fan because the letters were so small and light they would have blown out the window. Without the fan, we got so hot the letters stuck to us and we dripped on them. In spite of that, we got out several sets of these exhibits and they were the beginning of the splendid type now used by the Women's Bureau.

Besides trying to publicize the standards in every possible way, the Woman in Industry Service tried to find out through field investigations what was happening to women in the readjustment period after the war and we also started several investigations of women's employment in various states, which in the end became a major part of the program of the Women's Bureau.

The first of these investigations was made at the request of Governor James P. Goodrich of Indiana. This was the first time that the federal government had made a survey at the request of a state in order to give it the facts on women's employment. During later years we made the same type of survey in thirty-one other states. The facts we collected in these surveys were used as the basis for legislation and in many states laws were passed because of our findings.

That survey in Indiana had to be done in a hurry because the people interested wanted a report for the governor to send to the legislature, which was to meet the first part of January. We sent out a small number of field agents to get the information about working conditions and hours from the factories and working women of the state. They covered most of the industrial sections of the state, making factory inspections and having personal interviews with working women. When their reports came in, late in December, Miss van Kleeck got to

work on the final report and it was finished in the nick of
time. It was typical of the way we worked in those days that
I had to hold a taxi ticking at the entrance to the office while
the final pages of the report were typed before I could dash
off to get the train and carry the report to the governor.

I arrived in Indianapolis late on New Year's Day and the
next morning, with Mrs. Cox, who was head of the Indiana
bureau of women and children, I took the report to the governor. We wanted him, in his inaugural address to the legislature, to make some recommendations for labor legislation
for women. The governor was cordial, but said his speech
had already been written and that if we wanted to put a recommendation in it we would have to take it up with the man
who had written the speech for him. The governor then went
out to lunch, but we got hold of the man who had written
the speech, and in the governor's office we concocted a paragraph that was included in the speech, ending with the recommendation "that a law be passed making permanent the
Women's Division in the Inspection Department, regulating
the hours, and safeguarding the working conditions of women
in industry."

But Indiana was not ready to pass any legislation for
women. There was great opposition by the employers and
there had been no educational campaign among the general
public to tell them what it was all about. So nothing happened.

The Woman in Industry Service functioned until the early
spring of 1920 when a bill was passed by Congress creating
the Women's Bureau in the Department of Labor. Mary van
Kleeck wrote the bill which was introduced in the House by
Representative Philip Campbell from Kansas and in the Senate by Senator William Kenyon from Iowa. At the joint hearing of the House and Senate the bill had no opposition but,
instead, tremendous support. Almost every woman's organization then in existence testified for it.

One of the most important witnesses in favor of the bill

was Dr. Royal Meeker, head of the Bureau of Labor Statistics, who said his bureau could not make the investigations and gather the facts that we did and so it would not be a duplication of effort to have a women's bureau.

It was a fine hearing. It went on for two or three days and no one appeared in opposition. When Mr. Campbell was asked on the floor of the House, "What is this bureau going to do?" he said, "It is going to do what the bill says it is going to do!" and in due time the House acted favorably on the bill.

In the Senate, the opposition was led by Senator William King of Utah. A deal was made in the Senate that they would have a night session at which this bill was to be the only one brought up. Senator King and Senator Kenyon agreed that if Kenyon would not make a speech for it, King would not make one against it. Of course, Kenyon was asked questions by both sides and that gave him a chance to tell all about it, but King could not speak because of his agreement. The bill was passed in about fifteen minutes. I remember so well the night it was passed — June 20, 1920. Someone called me on the telephone about seven thirty and told me it was coming up. I got there a few minutes after the session started. Many of our friends, especially from the National Women's Trade Union League, were there looking on.

The league had done an outstanding job organizing support for the bill. Ethel Smith was the legislative representative of the national league in Washington and under her direction many of us were alerted when the bill was coming up in each house so that we could telephone friendly representatives and senators and ask them to be sure and be on the floor for the discussion and vote.

When the vote was over in the Senate I remember that we all went in to call on Senator Champ Clark. He sat there at his desk (he never got up for anyone) and his opening remark was, "What can you do for me, ladies?" We did not say it at the time, but we really felt that the establishment of the Women's Bureau as an agency of the federal government would do a great deal for every man and woman in the United States, because at last it was a matter of public record that women in industry were an important asset to the nation and that the federal government was ready to assume responsibility for their well-being.

14

Paris 1919

IN February 1919, when I was assistant director of the Woman in Industry Service, the labor organizations of all the Allied countries were holding a meeting in Paris with Samuel Gompers, president of the American Federation of Labor, as chairman. They were meeting to formulate a program for better standards of employment in the postwar period. We were very apprehensive because there were no women delegates to this conference. In fact, women were not represented at all. We had seen in the papers that Margaret Bondfield, secretary of the General Workers Union of England, had been in Paris and had talked to some of the British labor men but that she had not been invited to appear before the conference. We also heard that a group of women from the United States who were living in Paris at the time had appeared at the meeting, but we knew that they were not equipped to speak with any authority in behalf of working women.

At the same time the Peace Conference was going on in Paris and here again there was no one to speak for the interests of working women.

It seemed to us that it was very important to have some American labor women on the spot in Paris to present the standards that had been adopted at the last convention of the National Women's Trade Union League. Mrs. Robins was already working on this idea with officials at the White House and a number of influential people and, when President Wilson returned from his first trip to Paris, she got in touch with him. I supplemented her efforts by writing to the President asking if he did not think it would be a good idea to have representatives of women in Paris to present their problems and recommendations. He replied:

1 March, 1919

MY DEAR MISS ANDERSON:

I have your letter of yesterday and have read it not only with interest, but very thoughtfully, with regard to the question it asks.

I think it is very desirable that the women workers of the country should at least have one or two representatives in Paris, qualified to speak before the commissions that are considering labor matters. I am sorry to say that I am not informed as to whether any women's organizations are already represented over there or not. You will yourself be better informed about this than I am.

May I not thank you for your thoughtful kindness in consulting me?

Cordially and sincerely yours,
WOODROW WILSON

That letter settled it. Mrs. Robins had already decided that Rose Schneiderman, of New York, vice-president of the National Women's Trade Union League, and I should be the ones to go. I got leave of absence from the Woman in Industry Service and we started our preparations to get off. The Women's Trade Union League was to pay our expenses and had given us formal credentials and instructions and copies of the standards to be presented. My credentials said:

February 12, 1919

To the Members of the Peace Congress in Conference assembled.

GENTLEMEN:

We beg to advise you that Mary Anderson is a representative

of the National Women's Trade Union League of America. She is one of a mission elected to present to the Peace Congress the reconstruction program of the trade-union women of our country. She is Assistant Director of the Woman in Industry Service of the United States Department of Labor and a member of the Executive Board of the Boot and Shoe Workers Union. You are already familiar with our standards as cabled to you on February second. Every courtesy extended by you will be deeply appreciated not only by these delegates but also by the three hundred thousand working women whom they represent.

Yours very respectfully,
MARGARET DREIER ROBINS
(Mrs. Raymond Robins)
President
EMMA STEGHAGEN
Secretary-Treasurer

We had no difficulty in getting permission to go, or passports, or passage, but we were delayed somewhat because of a strike of the coal loaders. After a week's delay, we sailed to Halifax where we spent two or three days in the harbor coaling before we finally got off for England. The weather was terribly cold. Our ship had been used as a scout boat in the war and all the heating apparatus had been ripped out. Our only heat was from the little fireplace in the saloon.

I remember that among the passengers on the boat were Mme. Nellie Melba, the singer, and her pianist. She was very haughty to us and refused to sing for the Seamen's Benefit. There were not enough passengers on the boat to have a special train to London, which made Mme. Melba very angry. She came to us and said, "I think we ought to have a strike!" We asked what would be the point and how could we "strike," and she said, "We'll refuse to get off the boat!" We said we could not do that because we were in a hurry and were sure a train would come along in a few hours.

In London the first thing we did was to go to the police station to register. Stella Franklin had been able to get us a room at the Euston Hotel. That room was very cold. There was a fireplace, but when we asked to have a fire, they said we could not have one without a doctor's certificate. I caught a terrible cold, but it was too late by then to get a certificate and warm up.

We were in London for two or three days trying to get away. After hours and hours, we were able to get our visas and then we had to go to the police station again to tell them when we were leaving. During all this time there was snow, sleet, and very cold weather. We finally got away and crossed the channel on a boat that bobbed up and down all night. I was not seasick, but Rose was miserable. She lay on the floor, along with the others who were sick, and we were all very uncomfortable. The room seemed to have no air. I could not help thinking of the last journey I had made on a boat, thirty years before, when I left Sweden to come to the United States.

We finally got to Paris about half past two in the afternoon and, as we drew in, Rose said to me, "Aren't you thrilled about getting in to Paris?" But I answered, "No, I'm not thrilled about anything." My London cold had really made me sick.

From the train, we went to a restaurant and tried to order some food. There was a man from Idaho traveling with us, going over for the Red Cross, who went to the restaurant too. None of us could speak French and the waiter did not understand us, so we pointed to the things we wanted. The waiter kept saying something that sounded like "tickee, tickee." We could not imagine what he wanted until finally I remembered a little plate on the desk when we went through the customs with a sign saying, "Take three." I didn't know what they were, but I had taken three. I brought these out and the waiter was then satisfied. They were bread tickets.

After a night in a little hotel, where we finally got warm under a feather mattress, we ended up at the Petrograd Hotel, where Mary Dingman, an old friend of ours who was run-

ning the YWCA in Paris at that time, took care of us. We
were then among friends who could help us and since they
got their food from the United States commissary, it was a
little better than what we could get otherwise.

The first thing we did was to get in touch with the members of the American delegation to the Peace Conference who
were active in formulating policies. We had many meetings
with Dr. James I. Shotwell and with the members of the
English delegation, too.

At these meetings we discussed getting some phrase into
the constitution of the International Labor Organization stating that women, whenever possible, should be appointed as
advisory members to its conferences.

After we were assured that such a clause would be inserted
in the covenant, we were anxious to see President Wilson and
talk this over with him, knowing that he was interested and
thinking that he should know what we had recommended
and why. The President was ill at the time, and we waited
for his recovery. His physician, Dr. Cary Grayson, and his
publicity representative, Ray Stannard Baker, both told us
that as soon as he was well enough we should be the first to
see him.

After some days we learned that the President was up and
about. We thought we would get our appointment soon
and we started preparations for returning to the United States.
One of the things we had to do was to get, from the French
police court, permission to leave. At the court there were long
lines of people and the clerks followed the old method of
writing down everything in longhand. I was able to get
through in one morning, but Rose was not. Since we were
late for a meeting where we were to speak we had to leave.
When we went back the next day we wore our oldest clothes
because the place was so dirty. By twelve o'clock we had gotten Rose's permit and we stood wondering whether to have
lunch at the Galleries Lafayette or the Petrograd Hotel. We
voted for the latter because we could tell there what we were

getting as the menus were in English. When we arrived at the hotel the concierge flew past us shouting that the President wanted to see us at twelve thirty. It was then twelve twenty. The concierge was running for a taxi. It came quickly, and we got in just as we were, without even a chance to wash our hands.

The taxi went like lightning, but when we got to the Hotel Crillon, Ike Hoover, the President's chief usher, met us at the door saying, "Really, girls, you're late!" We explained and when we were taken into a room and the President came in, we explained again to him. He said, "Yes, I know, you don't have to apologize. That was my fault. I saw a place to put you in at the last moment and I did it." We were alone with him and told him our story. We asked that when the government delegates to the International Labor Organization were appointed one of them should be a woman. He said, "I think that is a quite reasonable request and when the time comes I'll give it more careful consideration. I will have it in mind."

Then we started to leave but he said, "Wait a minute. I want to talk with you about something. Do you feel as Gompers does about the Germans?" We said that we did not. Gompers had issued a terrific blast at the Germans through the newspapers in New York, but we felt that probably the Germans had learned a good deal. Also we were favorably impressed because we had heard that in their delegation to sign the peace treaty they were bringing women as well as men.

Then the President said, "Now I want to talk to you about something else. I want to tell you why I agreed to the French occupation of the Saar." He told us what the Germans had done to the mines, flooded them and destroyed their tonnage for years to come. He felt that in compensation it was no more than right that the French should have the coal from the Saar for a certain number of years after the war was over.

We told him that the labor movement in Paris had given

a dinner for us a few nights before, on which occasion the
French had toasted our President, and we said that we were
sure they were with him. He became somewhat excited,
moved to the edge of his chair, and said with emphasis, "I
think they are — I think they are."

That was the last time I ever saw President Wilson to speak
to, but in earlier conferences I had always found him very
sympathetic and understanding. I remember going to him
once with Agnes Nestor to talk about introducing a bill in
Congress for an eight-hour day. Congressman Edward Keating was to present this bill and we wanted the President's
support. We saw him in his office one afternoon. When we
came in he was writing at his desk but he got up and drew
up chairs and we sat around and talked. He said, "You don't
have to convince me because I am for the eight-hour day but
we have the question of constitutionality. The child labor
bill is now before the Supreme Court. Until we get that settled, we don't know whether such laws would be constitutional. But, in the meantime, if we can beat the devil around
the bush, we will beat him and I think Mr. Keating should
present the bill."

I think we laid the foundation in that trip to Paris for the
appointment of women on delegations to the International
Labor Organization. Although the United States did not associate itself with the International Labor Organization at first,
when we once began sending delegations there was always a
woman appointed. Perhaps that would have happened anyway, with the increasing prominence of women in political
life in the United States, but I am sure that the clause in the
constitution of the International Labor Organization saying,
"When questions especially affecting women are to be considered by the Conference, one at least of the advisers shall
be a woman," did have some effect although it was not nearly
as inclusive as we had hoped it would be.

While we were in Paris we made very interesting contacts
with the labor movement there. We were helped by a Mme.

Duchene, who spoke English; she put us in touch with the labor people and acted as our interpreter. We could not have gotten along without her. I think we must have gone to her house almost every day. We visited the labor headquarters and, at first, the people there were rather suspicious of us because they could not tell whether or not we were bona fide labor women. Luckily, we had our union cards and dues books with us and they could see from them who we really were.

At the end of our stay in Paris, the Central Labor Union gave us a banquet at their headquarters. It was a very fine party with hors d'oeuvres and champagne. Among the guests were three so-called labor leaders from the United States. One of them was a man named Sullivan, who, although he was Gompers' representative in Paris, was not very much of a trade union man. The other two he had brought with him were not labor men at all. One was a banker and the other was a young lawyer. I remarked to Mr. Sullivan that our hosts thought he was bringing bona fide labor people and he said that he had not explained at all whom he was bringing. I told Mme. Duchene who they were. The result was that the people who were running the dinner were furious and they put on a real communistic program, just to irritate the United States "labor men." It was Lenin and Trotsky every few minutes and I know they talked much more along those lines than they would have done at any other time.

Coming home about two in the morning, we took the banker and the lawyer in the taxi with us. The lawyer had been very taken with one of the young French women at dinner. He had asked if he could go home with her. She said he could not because her husband was meeting her right after the dinner. He told us this in the taxi. I said, "I think that you did not do the Americans credit when you made a suggestion like that. After all, these people are our hosts. They are respectable people and I think you had a great deal of nerve to talk in that way. I am thoroughly ashamed. One of

these days when you get convivial like this, you'll find someone who will take you up and then you'll be sorry."

On our return trip to the United States we stayed in England for about a week and saw something of the labor women
there. Margaret Bondfield, Mary Macarthur, and Stella
Franklin, all of whom I had known years before through the
Women's Trade Union League and at Hull House in Chicago, looked out for us and took us to meetings where we
learned something of what was going on.

But we did not have time for much because I had to get
home for the Boot and Shoe Workers' convention in Chicago.
Then in June, the National Women's Trade Union League
had a convention in Philadelphia. Margaret Bondfield and
Mary Macarthur came over from England for it and Rose
and I reported on our trip to Paris. As a conclusion to our
report we suggested that the league hold an international
labor conference of women.

Our experience in Paris and in London convinced us that
the time had come for labor women everywhere to get together and work together. We felt that a new era was ahead
of us and that this was the time to start women thinking and
acting on international matters. We were very hopeful when
the league voted to hold such a convention and Mrs. Robins
set to work to bring it about.

15

International Congresses of Working Women

THE First International Congress of Working Women was held in Washington in the autumn of 1919 at the same time as the first conference of the International Labor Office. We felt that this was a strategic time for our meeting because women were not properly represented at the labor conference and we wanted to inaugurate an international program for women and get it accepted by the conference.

We had a fine conference. Mrs. Robins had worked for months getting it organized and had put into it not only all her time and enthusiasm, but a great deal of money to finance the expenses of delegates who could not afford, in many cases, to meet the heavy costs of coming to the United States.

We had women representatives from Great Britain, Poland, France, Belgium, Sweden, Norway, Argentina, Canada, Czechoslovakia, and India. In addition, women visitors came from Cuba, Denmark, Japan, the Netherlands, Serbia, Spain, and Switzerland. I was secretary of the organizing committee for the conference and I will never forget my feelings when the meeting opened and I saw all those splendid women, from all over the world, come together to make plans for working women everywhere. Outstanding among the delegates were Mary Macarthur and Margaret Bondfield of Great Britain,

Jeanne Bouvier of France, Kirsten Hesselgren of Sweden, and Betzy Kjelsberg of Norway.

Mary Macarthur and Margaret Bondfield were old friends of ours. I first knew them when they came to Chicago in the old days. Mary had been secretary of the Women's Trade Union League of England and in that capacity had come several times to the United States. Margaret Bondfield made a good contrast to Mary, who was large, blonde, and a regular Britisher. Margaret, on the other hand, was small, dark, and very lively. She was an excellent speaker and could stir an audience with her eloquence and wit. She eventually became minister of labor in the first Labor government after World War I, and our friendship has continued throughout the years.

Jeanne Bouvier was a garment worker and became an inspector for the department of labor of the lingerie industry of France. She had written fine technical reports of that industry. She was small and a great talker, which rather complicated our proceedings because she spoke in French, which had to be interpreted. Later when I visited France she was always there to give me a friendly greeting.

Betzy Kjelsberg and Kirsten Hesselgren were favorites at the convention. I had never met Betzy before but she was a hearty soul and it did not take us long to get acquainted. She was for many years chief of the Women's Bureau in the Norwegian Department of Labor. Her bubbling sense of humor and her fluent English won the hearts of her American friends. Miss Hesselgren was an energetic, intelligent woman with lots of common sense. She became a leading statesman of Sweden and was a member of its Congress for twenty-one years, during which period most of the social legislation for Sweden was enacted.

Mrs. Robins presided over the meetings. We had big crowds because the convention was open to visitors and everyone was interested in the colorful group of delegates.

I think the conference was especially successful because

all the delegates were bona fide representatives of their countries and knew what they were talking about, because the subject matter of the conference was limited to the special problems of working women, and, lastly, because the conference was not just a "flash in the pan" but resulted in a continuing organization. I think all these things are necessary if a conference is to amount to anything more than a "talk fest." I have been to so many women's conferences where everything in the world was discussed and resolved about by women who were appointed delegates chiefly because they had the money to come but who really knew nothing about the people they were supposed to speak for and had no way of following up the fine resolutions that were passed. It has always seemed to me that except for the value of publicity at the time and the personal contacts made, this type of meeting is not worth the money and effort put into it. But this was not the case with the First International Congress of Working Women.

That conference had a lasting effect. There were plenty of problems but on the whole the delegates were almost unanimous in their recommendations. We formulated international standards for the employment of women and forwarded them to the International Labor Conference, where they were adopted almost word for word. The women's conference also had a stimulating effect on all of us, particularly on the women from the European countries where the standards of living were so low and there was almost no organization.

This kind of conference was a brand-new experience for many of the women who came. Some of them had their difficulties. If their delegation included representatives of their government, they did not always feel free to act as they wanted to. For some of the women, the conference opened up an entirely new field of work on their return home.

I remember especially the delegate from Japan, Mme. Tanaka. She was the wife of a professor at the Tokyo University and had been appointed by the government as an adviser to represent women at the International Labor Conference and as a delegate to the International Congress of Working Women. She had studied in the United States and knew the language well. The Japanese government, in choosing their delegates for the International Labor Conference, did not let the trade union movement select representatives, but appointed as the workers' delegate the superintendent of a large shipyard. This was not in conformance with the International Labor Organization constitution agreed upon, which was that workers should nominate their representatives, and it was a great source of irritation among the workers in Japan. I heard that when the delegation sailed for the United States the workers appeared at the dock wearing shrouds.

After she was appointed an adviser someone remarked to Mme. Tanaka that she was going to the United States to represent the workers but that she did not know them or their problems. She realized that this was true so she got in touch with a young worker named Ogota. They had a long talk and the longer they talked the more Mme. Tanaka realized she did not know anything about the workers' problems. She then persuaded the government to appoint Ogota to go with her and they were always together at our conference.

When I first saw Ogota, in front of the Washington Hotel, she was so shy that she stood with her face to the wall. In spite of this, she was a great help to Mme. Tanaka and her shyness wore off until just before they left she made a speech at a meeting of the Women's Trade Union League saying that when she got back to Japan she was going to organize the women workers there.

One day, in the committee on women in industry of the International Labor Conference, Mme. Tanaka told the committee members what very bad conditions for working women existed in Japan, particularly in the textile industry. The Japanese government delegate reported this to the rest of his delegation and they did not like it at all.

Shortly after this Mme. Tanaka came to me and said, "I

have been put off the delegation and have been prohibited from going to any of the meetings. The excuse is that I am pregnant. I am, but I know it is just an excuse. I suppose it is because I exposed the working conditions of women in Japan." She asked what I could do for her.

Mrs. Robins decided that she and I would ask for an appointment with the Japanese delegation; she would tell them that we had heard the story and that it was not true that in America women who are pregnant should not be seen in public. We finally got an appointment and they bowed all over the place. Mrs. Robins told them that we knew Mme. Tanaka was pregnant and that that was nothing against her, that, in fact, we were proud of women who were pregnant and did not restrict their activities. Our pleading was successful and about a day later Mme. Tanaka was back as an adviser. This broke the ice in the Japanese delegation and finally the labor delegate made a speech and pointed to the Japanese flag as the flag of the country that exploited workers more than any other in the world. When the conference was over he asked Mrs. Robins and me to a special dinner in our honor. There were many guests from other countries and the room was literally filled with chrysanthemums. It was one of the most beautiful dinners I have ever attended and it was all because of what we had done for Mme. Tanaka.

After she went back to Japan I did not hear from her for about a year. Finally I heard indirectly that she had been very ill and had lost her baby, which had been a great blow to her. When I did get a letter from her, she told me this was true and that she had not recovered entirely. I felt, reading between the lines, that her husband was not pleased with what she had done in this country and that she had been greatly criticized. I had another letter later on in which she said Ogota had been very active in the trade union movement but she did not say with what success.

One of the results of the First International Congress of Working Women was a permanent international organization that was to carry on a continuing program and hold regular international conferences of working women. Mrs. Robins was elected president and Maud Swartz, a member of the Typographical Union, was secretary. The headquarters were in the office of the National Women's Trade Union League in Chicago.

We all had great hopes for this organization and Mrs. Robins put almost all her time and money into it. But, unfortunately, it had a very short life. The next conference was held in Geneva with Mrs. Robins, Emma Steghagen, Maud Swartz, and Sarah Green as United States delegates. The third meeting was held in Vienna in 1923. We had a good many delegates there — Mrs. Robins, Mary Dreier, Agnes Nestor, Agnes Johnson, Elisabeth Christman, Maud Swartz, Frieda Miller, Rose Schneiderman, Pauline Newman, and I.

The discussions at the Vienna meeting were very interesting. They covered almost every problem that affected women as citizens or as workers. Women's work toward peace was the first topic for discussion and the conference went on record for a revision of the Versailles treaty; it condemned the occupation of the Ruhr; it upheld the policy of settling all international questions by open negotiation, an international court, and a league of nations with necessary jurisdiction; and it recommended the cancellation of inter-Allied debts provided steps toward disarmament were agreed upon.

In the field of industrial conditions the delegates studied the work of the International Labor Office and reported on the progress of the ratifications of the various conventions on such subjects as child labor, the eight-hour day, labor laws for women, agricultural labor problems, unemployment, industrial homework, and many other industrial issues. On the issue of labor laws specifically affecting women the conference took the position that any industrial group, whether men or women, should be its own judge of the way to secure better industrial standards — by trade union agreement alone, by legislation, or by both methods. Its resolution on this subject stated that it was "in favor of labor legislation for women in countries where the organized working women wish to use this method to improve the industrial conditions." Regulation of homework, family allowances — meaning an addition to the basic wage of a man according to the number of his dependents — and methods of organizing women into trade unions were also thoroughly discussed, and many different points of view were presented by the delegates from different countries.

It was all most interesting, but in spite of the fine program and the importance of the things we were considering, it ended by being a very unhappy meeting.

At the Geneva conference Marian Phillips, one of the English delegates, had been made secretary of the organization. She had not done a great deal of work between conferences and she and Margaret Bondfield and some others felt that they really could not carry on with things as they were. They wanted us to transform our organization into a women's committee of the International Federation of Trade Unions. Mrs. Robins was very much opposed to this and most of us were with her. We knew that a women's committee within the International Federation of Trade Unions would not be free to act in the way we thought we must and, besides, since our trade union movement in the United States was not a part of the International Federation, the Women's Trade Union League, which was affiliated with the trade union movement in the United States, could not be a part of the International Federation either.

There was a great deal of agitation about this for a year before the Vienna conference. Maud Swartz, a member of the Typographical Union in the United States and president of the New York Women's Trade Union League, was strongly in favor of our merging with the International Federation of Trade Unions. She conducted a vigorous campaign in the United States among the members of the league and bitter feelings were stirred up.

The meeting in Vienna was very turbulent, but in the end it was voted to turn the organization over to the International Federation of Trade Unions. This was a great blow to all of us. The Women's Trade Union League had put a great deal of money and effort into the organization, which had promised to be very successful, but when this decision was made we had to withdraw and our dream of a real international organization of working women was over.

I think our efforts came to nothing chiefly because of a lack of understanding of each other's problems. In some of the European countries, particularly England, women were much more integrated in the labor movement than we were. The delegates from these countries did not realize how much on the fringe we in America still were and they were so busy within their own organizations that they did not have the time to spend on ours. Also they did not know enough about the labor union setup in the United States and the position of the National Women's Trade Union League to realize that we could not act independently of the American Federation of Labor if we were to retain our position in the United States. The European delegates knew that if they voted in favor of merging with the International Federation of Trade Unions we would have to withdraw but they would not admit it. Margaret Bondfield and others suggested that we would be able to appoint and send some kind of committee to the federation but when I said that not one of us could be appointed or could serve when our own unions were not affiliated, the answer was, "We have to look out for Europe. You are too far away. We haven't got time to go along with organizations like yours."

For a long time after this we never mentioned the Vienna conference to Mrs. Robins because she was so upset about it. I think the results of this conference had a very deteriorating effect on the whole women's trade union movement. The women at our international conferences were able and respected and the action we took was really significant, but afterward the women's committee in the International Federation of Trade Unions was completely subordinated, as we had said it would be. When the women's committee met, their meetings were presided over by a man who did not let them take up a question unless it had been put on the agenda before the meeting.

I attended one of their meetings when I was in Geneva at the conference of the International Labor Organization in 1931. It was pathetic. I remember that some of the younger women from Germany were there and they certainly told the presiding officer what they thought of the situation. They protested that the committee was useless and they suspected that they had been appointed just as figureheads. They said that the problem was to organize women, but that this committee had no way of doing the work, that all they did was make recommendations and have discussions but there was no action and no funds to enable them to take action. The man who was presiding acted as if what they were talking about did not mean a thing. The meeting was really only a gesture. It was the same old idea of putting women on the side, forming a committee at which they could talk, and then not paying any more attention to them.

All through my life I have found that this attitude is the most difficult thing women have to contend with. The situation is better now, but still there seems to be a general feeling that women should be segregated in the work of the world and that they should have a say only in so-called "women's problems." The person who decides what is a woman's problem is usually a man who does not want to bother with it. The really important problems are kept for the men to solve while the women are shunted off onto minor committees on "matters of interest to women." I do not know of any matter that is not of interest to women, who are, after all, people and citizens. I hope that in the years to come this will be realized by women as well as men and that women will eventually come into their own.

16

Activities of the Bureau

BY the time the First International Congress of Working Women was held I had become director of the Woman in Industry Service following Mary van Kleeck's resignation in July 1919. I took over this job with a good many misgivings. Although I had learned a great deal from Mary about how to administer the service, I knew that it was going to be difficult and I was rather appalled by the prospect. I could never have done the job if it had not been for the help I got from the other members of the staff and from Mary van Kleeck herself, who kept in touch with our work at first and helped me whenever I needed her.

From the very earliest days of the service I felt that I had many friends among the employees. (I did not bring into the service or, later on, into the Women's Bureau any of my former friends and associates — for no special reason but just because it did not work out that way. The positions were all under civil service and it so happened that none of my friends took the civil service examination.) Throughout the years in the Women's Bureau I always felt that we were a very closely knit organization, working together for the best interests of working women. When I took over we had fewer than twenty employees. When I left the Women's Bureau there were about sixty people on the staff. Our appropriation had increased from $30,000 to $246,000. But, whatever the size of the staff, I always tried to keep in touch with all of them. I felt that their work was just as important as mine because after all it was a part of the whole job we were all doing together. Throughout the years they were not only hard working and extremely competent, but, more important still, they were loyal and dedicated to the cause of improving conditions for working women.

By the time Mary van Kleeck left, the pattern of work for the Woman in Industry Service had been laid out. Her greatest accomplishment was the adoption of the standards, which became the guide for the entire country in matters of women's employment. She had also established the techniques of investigation which have been followed by the Women's Bureau ever since. The importance placed on home visits and individual contacts with the workers as well as personal interviews with employers, in addition to detailed collection of payroll data, made the reports of conditions in various industries accurate and illuminating. The success of these techniques is indicated by the fact that our conclusions were never challenged throughout the period in which I was director of the bureau. Mary also started the program of information and education through popular exhibits, which was greatly enlarged and developed in later years and was of real service in rallying all interested organizations to support improvements in women's employment.

There was never any great difference between the program of the Women's Bureau and the program that was started by the Woman in Industry Service. After the service was put on a permanent basis and renamed the Women's Bureau, we followed the pattern initiated by the service. Of course, there was a change of emphasis from year to year as one problem or another seemed more acute and had to be dealt with. The small appropriations for the service and the bureau limited our activities so that we had to select carefully the most important subjects to concentrate on each year, but the service and the bureau were established "to formulate standards and policies which shall promote the welfare of wage earning women, improve their working conditions, increase their efficiency and advance their opportunities for profitable employment." In doing this we stuck pretty much to the same techniques throughout the time I was in charge of the work.

I think the most important thing we did was to assemble as much general information as we could get to show actual conditions of women's employment, their wages, and hours. Starting with the state survey of women's employment made in Indiana during the first months of the Woman in Industry Service, we had made investigations of this sort in thirty-two states by the time I left the Women's Bureau. We never made a state survey unless we were asked to do so by the state authorities or by responsible organizations in a state. We had no legal power to examine the records and conditions but we were always able to get the cooperation of the employers and usually we found them most helpful and willing to give our agents every facility for their work. It was very important for us to have this kind of cooperation because without it we could not have done much.

From the very beginning we decided that if our reports were to be of any real use they must be based on the actual facts and not on generalizations or hearsay evidence. When we wanted to find out what women's wages were we did not take the statements of an employer or of a woman herself. Instead, we sent our agents into a plant and they copied the exact records from the payrolls. For every investigation that included wages we collected thousands and thousands of these payroll records, which later were assembled and analyzed by our statistical division. This information was always supplemented by personal interviews with the women themselves.

I think getting these personal interviews was the toughest part of the work of our field agents, but it was very important. These interviews gave us much information about the problems and conditions in the various industries that would not show up in any records. It was a hard job and I always felt sorry for the agents who had to do the home visiting. They would get the names and addresses of the women from the employers or from the unions and other agencies in the state. Then would start the grind of making home visits because, of course, the women could not be interviewed while they were at work. That would have interfered with production and we did not think they would feel free to talk frankly. We had to search them out in their homes, in the evenings after working hours or on Sundays.

It was the same kind of thing I used to do when I was organizing and I knew how wearing it was. I remember very well doing home visiting once in Baltimore. Many of the houses in Baltimore are built with wooden front steps that can be detached and carried away for painting and repairs. The steps are almost always painted white and the women have the back-breaking job of scrubbing these steps every week to keep them clean and white. Often I would come to a house when the steps had been removed. I could not reach up from the ground to knock or ring the bell (if there was one) and I would have to go through the alley to the rear door. In those days there was usually open sewage that ran in a gutter through the alleys and it was not pleasant. When the door was opened I would ask for a certain person and say that I would like to talk to her about her conditions of work. They would be skeptical in many instances but usually they saw I was a worker like themselves, took me into the house, and though they might be hostile at first, in the end we would talk things over and become friends.

It is the most wearing job there is. You really have to force yourself to go to the house and try to make the contact, not knowing what kind of reception you will get and not knowing whether the interview will be helpful or not. I was a rather shy person and it was very difficult for me to barge in on someone else, but I did it and later on I appreciated the way our agents stuck to it and brought us such valuable information.

In this way we built up a mass of exact information about the conditions of women's employment and our reports were used very widely in the states, usually as a basis for legislation to improve conditions.

In addition to these general surveys, there were always special problems cropping up that had to be studied. Sometimes we initiated special studies on our own responsibility but more often we undertook them at the request of one group or another that wanted specific data.

One of my biggest problems always was how to spread our appropriation so that we could do the most effective work. I know that a great many people thought we should adopt a program, deciding what we should do, and stick to it. But I always felt that we had been set up to serve the people of the United States and if we got requests from responsible groups to investigate certain subjects we should do all we could to get the information for them. The result was that our program from year to year was a compromise. Part of our appropriation was spent on getting information and developing educational programs about situations that we knew were important and that needed continuous attention. The rest of the appropriation was used for special studies made at the request of states or of organizations.

Naturally this led to a good deal of criticism from both sides. The organizations that worked with the Women's Bureau and helped us to get larger appropriations from Congress often suggested that we should announce a big project for which they could "go to bat" with the Appropriations committees in Congress. I never did that, because I did not feel I could risk tying up the main part of our appropriation for one or two projects when I knew that so many local and state organizations and special groups were going to need our help. I think that if a government agency is going to keep alive and in touch with the times it must be in a position to

respond to special situations and it must not set itself up to dic-
tate what should and should not be done. We tried to work
with everyone who was genuinely interested in improving
conditions for women workers and at the same time we tried
to point out the biggest and most important problems, the
actual facts, and the possible solutions.

It would be tedious to mention all the subjects that we
delved into during the years I was with the bureau. The
annual reports and the reports of our investigations show that
far better than I can. But it is worth while to mention a few
of the subjects that were with us and on our minds during
all those years.

Perhaps the most familiar and exasperating problem of any
working woman is the famous (or should I say infamous?)
"pin money" theory. This theory, which has been advanced
as long as women have been working, is that women only
work for "pin money" and have no family responsibilities. Of
course it is not true, but it has been so widely circulated and
accepted that I think it is the chief cause of the low wages
of women in comparison with men. It is an infuriating theory
to anyone who knows anything about women workers.

One of the first things we did in the Women's Bureau was
to make a thorough investigation of the share of wage-earning
women in family support. This investigation showed what a
great part working women were playing in supporting their
families and themselves. It showed how many times it took
more than the husband's or father's wages to support the
family. It showed how many girls were sending money home
or turning over their whole pay envelopes to their families.
It showed how married women carried the double job of
homemaker and wage earner so that their families could have
a little better education, medical care, or higher standards of
living. I myself knew what this problem was. I had my sister's
family to help. Her husband was dead, she had no one else
to help her, and she had a daughter to bring up. She worked
sometimes, doing housework, but it was so hard on her that

she could not stand it for long and would have to quit. What I earned was the only regular money that came into the home. I found that almost every woman I knew had someone dependent upon her and I do not think that many of us ever felt there was much security in life. Even I, with a good job in the government, did not know when an administration changed whether or not I would be able to keep on. So, while my income was much higher than most working women's, at the same time I never felt secure. I had obligations that I had to use my money for and I had my own living expenses, but I tried to be as economical as possible so that I would have something if I did not keep my job. It was only in the latter years, after my sister died, that I was able to save money and buy annuities.

When I came into the government service I started in the Ordnance Department at a salary of $2000 a year. This was a much higher income than I had ever had before. But it cost more to live in Washington and to keep up my home in Chicago. At first I only came to Washington for three months and since I did not think I would be away longer than that, my Chicago apartment had to be paid for and I had to see that my sister was cared for. She was very ill at the time with a broken hip.

Then, when the Woman in Industry Service was formed, my salary was increased to $3500 a year. I was pleased about that, but I did not feel that my financial worries were over because I still had my future to think about. After Miss van Kleeck left and I became director, my salary went up to $5000. That was better still, but there was always lurking in the back of my mind the question "How long?" Eventually my salary went up to $7500 and at last I felt secure, because with fewer responsibilities I was able to save and buy annuities. But this did not come for a long time. I never worked for "pin money" and I think I resented this theory more than any of the other misstatements that were so often made about women in industry.

Because we knew it was so important, the Woman in Industry Service and the Women's Bureau never gave up collecting facts to disprove this theory. We made more than one special investigation about it and besides, whenever we made a wage study, we put in a section on the home responsibilities of the women. We made special studies of married working women which added important facts to our records. We hammered away on this subject for twenty-five years but I do not think the job is finished yet. I even had an argument about it with Frances Perkins when she was secretary of labor. She had mentioned the subject in her annual report and she said to me that there were many women who just worked for "pin money." She had been questioned about this by one of the newspaperwomen and I said, "I can well understand that, because these newspaperwomen know from their own lives that it is not the case. Long before the Women's Bureau was started, we had that theory to contend with and we knew that it was a terrible charge to make about working women. I thought we had laid that ghost."

This attitude toward women workers has come down through the ages and I am afraid that there are still many people who feel that women should not be working outside their homes. The question is still asked, "Why don't women stay at home and wash the dishes?" It seemed at times as if it did no good for us to say that if they did not go out to work there would be no dishes to wash.

In spite of all the facts we gathered on this subject there are still some ill-advised people who keep on trying to rake up the old pin money theory. But on the whole I think we have proved through careful fact finding that women are part of the whole industrial system and that they have to be such in order that they themselves and those who are dependent on them may live.

17

Equal Pay for Women

NEXT to getting the facts about women's employment and trying to lay the ghost of the pin money theory, I think one of the most important issues that the Women's Bureau worked on was equal pay for women and men. From the very beginning of the Woman in Industry Service we said that wages should be based on the job content and not on the sex of the worker. We said this in the first standards issued and we have been saying it ever since. I think we have made some progress in getting this principle accepted but it has been slow, hard work and is not nearly finished yet.

In the early days, when we first issued the standards, we put in a statement on wages that said, "Wages shall be established on the basis of occupation and not on the basis of sex or race." But although this standard had the force of an official recommendation by the federal government, there was not much chance of its being adopted. A good many people endorsed it who did not really agree with it.

We always tried to push equal pay, but we ran into a great deal of opposition from employers, labor unions, and labor in general. I think the men always felt that they were inferior if they did not get more than the women and they did not realize that if they permitted lower wage rates for women the next thing that would happen would be that women would replace men because they were cheaper. Even if an employer theoretically accepted the policy of "equal pay for equal work" it did not do much good because he might then say that what the women were doing was not exactly the same as what the men were doing, so the women were paid less. In many factories there is a well-defined rule as to what is men's work and what is women's work. Even when the workers are all on piecework the rates are much lower for the women than for the men. This inequality applies to white-collar workers as well as to workers in industry. It is a matter of prejudice that is very hard to overcome. The women themselves present a problem. They do not have very strong bargaining power. Most of them are not organized. When they are organized they do not have much influence in most of their unions. They have to get a job and they are not in a position to stand out for "equal pay." They must take what they can get.

One of our great problems has been how to formulate a statement on equal pay that would be really enforceable. The simple slogan "Equal pay for equal work" we found did not mean much when we came to apply it in a practical way. There are too many possibilities of evasion. It really requires a job analysis of each operation in a plant to show that women are or are not doing the same work as men. The unions are not equipped to do this and it is not likely that employers will do it either. If there is to be any law or union agreement on this matter, it must be carefully phrased so that a job analysis is not necessary.

Our first real advance on the equal pay front came in the days of the National Recovery Administration, which was set up during the depression to secure the cooperation of employers and workers in raising standards of wages and hours and working conditions. To this end code authorities were established for each industry and after prolonged hearings and negotiations with workers and employers specific codes were adopted. Industries that followed these codes were entitled to display the emblem of the National Recovery Administration, a blue eagle. It was through these hearings and discussions that the people in general began to understand that women are a part of the industrial setup and should not be used to depress wage standards. I think the labor men got a great deal of enlightenment from the National Recovery Administration, and learned a lot about other industries as well as their own.

When the National Recovery Administration was first being put into effect I got in touch with members of the committees working on standards for each industry, particularly in the women-employing industries, William Green, John L. Lewis, and others. Lewis was then head of the CIO. It was very interesting to see him when he found the low wages and the poor conditions in certain of the industries, particularly where women were employed. He was very perturbed. He had worked closely with the miners and knew their problems but had not had much time for other industries. By organizing the CIO he found out what was going on in other industries and he began a real crusade to raise the standards of work. He always helped us.

We had plenty of friends in the National Recovery Administration. Leo Wolman was appointed by the secretary of labor as the executive secretary of the Labor Division and Rose Schneiderman was also in the division. But most of the labor men and women could not give full time to the work of the NRA; they could only be present for meetings and they had so much to do with the industrial committees that they had little control over the general policies.

I had one of the people from our office go every morning to the National Recovery Administration to find out what hearings were coming up and to ask if we could be heard. Then, when she came back, we would write a statement that one of us would present to the committee holding a hearing. The purpose of these hearings was to help employers and employees to set up minimum standards, acceptable to both, on hours, wages, and certain conditions of employment. One of the problems taken up by the committees was the theory that competition of women with men lowered the men's wages. The Women's Bureau was the only place where there was much information on that score.

After the hearings were completed and a code adopted for the industry the National Recovery Administration put out the blue eagles to be given to the employers to show that they had set certain standards of employment and were trying to live up to them. Before they set the standards for the blue eagles in the industries where mostly women were employed, I was asked to agree to them.

I remember that once the laundry committee wanted me to accept five or six dollars a week as a wage for women. I would not agree, saying that I could never accept a standard of that kind. I could not understand how the government could set such a standard. They called and called me by telephone, but I would not change my mind. Then the next thing I heard was that Leo Wolman had signed the agreement. I went to the secretary of labor to ask her to protest. She was not in, but her secretary, Miss Jay, called Wolman, who said that he did not know much about it. His secretary had signed it and he had not looked into it at all. It was an "automatic" signing.

Miss Jay said, "Miss Anderson does not agree. She is here now. Would you like to speak to her?" He replied, "No, I'll withdraw that signature."

There were many crosscurrents of that kind, particularly where women were concerned, and we had to be constantly on the alert. One day one of the labor men from the heavy industries came to me and said, "You and Miss Christman object to women getting less wages than men. Our hearings on that are tomorrow morning and I expect you to be over to put up a real fight."

We went and made our objections. There were ten thousand women in the heavy industries and the suggestion was that the minimum wage should be set at forty cents an hour for the men and thirty-five cents an hour for the women, although the women were doing almost the same work. We protested against that.

The man who presided over the meeting turned to me and said, "Now I am in a dilemma. What would you do? I can get forty cents an hour for men and thirty-five cents an hour for women and there are women in this industry who are only getting eighteen cents an hour. Isn't that a pretty good raise? Shall I let the men go down to thirty-five cents an hour, or take forty cents for the men and thirty-five cents for the women?"

I said, "That is a hard question, when you put it that way, but I am afraid that is not all there is to it. There ought to be the same wage. I think it would be better for industry as well as the workers if they were all paid the same."

They finally permitted forty cents for the men and thirty-five cents for the women. The labor man was with them. He let us have our say but he did not back us up a bit. Nevertheless, we were able, because of our consistent nagging, to get the same minimum for women in about seventy-five per cent of the codes and in the others we were able to get the differential decreased.

This work took almost all our time because we were constantly making investigations to find what the differentials were and many times we had to send out an agent to get spot information for the hearings on the codes. In the bureau, almost our whole Division of Research worked on this question.

The women workers themselves were not at all prepared to argue their case and the National Women's Trade Union League did a great deal to help. Elisabeth Christman worked on certain code authorities herself, especially the glove workers' code authority, and she worked and helped in general, speaking before industrial committees and often using our information. She and the bureau both helped the women prepare cases, notified them of the hearings, and assisted wherever we could. Many of the women's organizations too, especially the YWCA and the League of Women Voters, did a great deal, speaking before the authorities and keeping very close to the general staff to see what was going on and giving what information they had.

After the National Recovery Administration came the Walsh-Healy Act, which gave us another opportunity to raise pay rates for women. This act, passed in 1936, was really the entering wedge for the federal Wage and Hour Law that followed in 1938. The Walsh-Healy Act gave to the Department of Labor the power to set up standards of employment in the production of materials produced under contract with the federal government. I think this act had a tremendous effect on women's employment. The Women's Bureau made a number of surveys, particularly in the garment industry, for the Contract Division of the department and our findings were used by the industry committee called by the Contract Division to set minimum wages. The employers would attack us but our facts always stood up. It was a different kind of work from what we had been doing and it was not easy for our investigators, but I was sure they were very happy to see that our investigations were being so useful and that the bureau was getting more recognition.

Then came the federal Wage and Hour Law in which we really made some progress. This act set standards of minimum wages and maximum hours for workers employed in the manufacture of goods used in interstate commerce. I think I had a good deal to do with getting into that law the statement in connection with fixing wage orders that "No classification shall be made under this section on the basis of age or sex." It was an anxious time for me while the hearings on the bill were going on. The secretary of labor was going to appear and the solicitor of the department, Gerard Reilly, was working up her testimony. I talked to him and said, "Well, Gerry, I think we had better put in something for her to say about the same minimum for men and women."

He put in a bit, about two lines. When I went to the committee hearing the day she was going to testify the women of the press came up to me and asked what she was going to say about the same minimum for men and women. I answered, "Well, I know it is in her testimony and she will speak about it but you will have to wait and hear what it is." Unfortunately, when she came to that part she left out the two lines and went on to the next paragraph.

When the hearing was over, I nearly died because not a word had been said about the same minimum for men and women. The newspaperwomen all rushed up to me and asked why she had left that out. I answered, "God knows! Go up and ask her." But before they got a chance to, Senator Robert La Follette asked if she did not think that women should have the same minimum as men. She said, "Yes," and I heaved a sigh of relief. As she went out she said to me, "I fixed that all right, didn't I? It was such a long statement that I couldn't read it all." It was all right in the end, but I could not help feeling discouraged that she had picked those two lines to leave out.

All through the time she was secretary of labor, I think Miss Perkins rather minimized the importance of women's problems because she knew that a good many of the representatives of organized labor did not like her very well, partly because she was a woman and partly because they thought of her as a social worker and not a real labor person. So every time there was a chance to single out women, she leaned over backward not to do it. I understood her difficulties and sympathized with her, but just the same it was discouraging not to have more enthusiastic backing.

The result of the inclusion of the clause on the same minimum for men and women in the Wage and Hour Law was that later on when committees met to set higher minimums than were in the act itself, there was never any question of a differential for women, because it was in the law that there should not be any.

Our next major victory in the equal pay battle came during World War II, when the unions finally negotiated an agreement with General Motors, approved by the War Labor Board, which stipulated that there should be no differential for women and awarded considerable sums in back pay to women who had been paid lower rates. It took a great deal of work to achieve this. The Women's Bureau sent agents into the plants to get the facts and to persuade the union leaders that it would be to their advantage to insist on the abolition of the differential. I got my old friend and associate Elisabeth Christman to take leave for a year from her work as secretary-treasurer of the National Women's Trade Union League and come to the Women's Bureau to head this work. She accomplished it with great distinction and I think her tact and enthusiasm and her great knowledge of trade union negotiation had much to do with the success of our efforts.

The principle of equal pay for women got a further boost at the meeting of the International Labor Office held in Philadelphia in 1944. The charter that was adopted at that time included a clause saying: "The redistribution of women workers in each national economy should be carried out on the principle of complete equality of opportunity for men and women in respect of admission to employment on the basis of their individual merit, skill and experience, and steps should be taken to encourage the establishment of wage rates on the basis of job content, without regard to sex."

The wording was our own and was so carefully drawn that no one could object to it. I think the adoption of this principle by an international organization like the International Labor Organization will have a very good effect. I know, however, that resolutions and agreements are not enough to wipe out these age-old discriminations against women. Legislation is necessary too. Five states have already passed equal pay laws and though enforcement is spotty, the principle has been established. I am now working on a bill in Congress for equal pay for women employed in interstate commerce. We have great hopes for this bill. When it is passed it will affect a large number of women and we hope it will be followed by state action that will require equal pay for the women who do not come under the federal law.

18

Discriminations against Women

IN all the phases of our work during the whole time I was with the Women's Bureau we had to be on the alert to fight discriminations against women. One of them was unequal pay but there were others too. Sometimes these discriminations hit us in the bureau itself and made it much more difficult to carry on our program.

One of the most serious situations we had to face came in the very early days after the Women's Bureau was established when Senator Reed Smoot of Utah put a proviso in our appropriation bill saying that only two people on the staff could be paid more than two thousand dollars a year. He said that no woman on earth was worth more than that. I was aghast at this, knowing how it would affect us, because we had several people, our most valued workers, who were paid more than two thousand dollars. I went to Mr. Smoot myself and told him, thinking that he would listen to a businesslike statement, that no business could operate that way and that if this proviso stood we would lose some of our best people. He laid his hand on my shoulder and said, "You needn't worry. You won't lose anyone. After the war we'll have so much unemployment they'll take the positions at any price." As it happened, he was right. A few of our best people had private incomes and did not have to depend entirely on their salaries.

They made the sacrifice for the good of the bureau and stayed on at lower salaries until the matter was adjusted a couple of years later by the Reclassification Act.

All through my life it has been my experience that this is the kind of thing women have to accept and put up with again and again, if they are going to get a chance to do anything. I myself did it for a good many years while I was the only unpaid member of the executive board of the International Boot and Shoe Workers Union. I think that if I had made an issue of it I might have been paid as the other members were, but I did not want to jeopardize the opportunity I had to represent women on this board, so I let it go.

When we began to look into discriminations against women in the government service, we found that there was a very serious problem. There was great dissatisfaction among the women employees of the government because they were prohibited by the Civil Service Commission from taking certain examinations. At the request of the Federation of Federal Employees, one of the first studies made by the Women's Bureau, in September 1919, was a survey of the examinations open to women and the comparative salaries of the men and women appointed. Our survey showed that women were excluded from sixty per cent of the examinations, and that the prevailing entrance salary paid to women was very much lower than for men in the same grade.

Because we found such a great discrepancy, we thought it best to have a conference with the Civil Service Commission before we published the report. When the facts were pointed out the commission immediately issued an order that all the examinations be opened to both men and women. Thus we accomplished our purpose before the report was published and were able to say in the published report that this discrepancy had been done away with, at least as far as taking the examinations was concerned. But it was another question when it came to appointments because it was up to the appointing officer to state whether he wanted men or women.

There also remained a great difference between the salaries paid to men and women.

Later on, I remember, some of the Woman's party members came to me and wanted me to support a bill to take away the right of the appointing officer to stipulate whether he wanted a man or a woman and oblige him to select from the three persons with the highest rating on the civil service list. At the Senate hearing on this bill, the civil service commissioner, Martin A. Morrison, said that because of the Veterans Preference Act veterans could qualify with much lower ratings than anyone else on the list and they would have to have preference. Almost all the veterans were men, and if we took away the rights of the appointing officers to choose, a woman would not be appointed in the government service for the next fifty years. I agreed with that argument and was glad that the bill did not pass.

When the Reclassification Act was passed in 1923, qualifications and salaries for the grades were set irrespective of sex, which eliminated the discrimination against women and we thought we had finally settled this issue so far as government jobs were concerned. But some years later, one of the civil service commissioners, Jessie Dell, a member of the Woman's party, felt that women should try again to take away the right of the appointing officer to designate whether he wanted men or women. I pointed out that we still had the Veterans Preference Act and that I, who always wanted women, would probably have to take veterans instead. Nevertheless, she kept pushing that point and when Mr. Hoover came in as president she persuaded him to issue a presidential order to take away the right of the appointing officer to choose men or women. That operated for about a year until there was a change of administration. Then some of us were able to get President Roosevelt to countermand the order because, as it worked out, it resulted in a great discrimination against women.

I think that the Veterans Preference Act is really very dangerous to the government service. I feel very sympathetic with the veteran wanting a job when he comes back and I believe that those who were in government service when they left should have their jobs back if they want them and if they are able to hold them. But to give general preference to all veterans has a very bad effect on civil service. It almost nullifies the civil service laws.

I think the government has an obligation to the civilian population to employ qualified people, because if the government employs those who are not qualified for the jobs the work will be done very badly and the whole country will suffer as a result. If we mean what we say, that we want employees in government selected by civil service examinations and not by patronage, then I think we should support the civil service to the fullest extent. Our trouble is that, after a great war, the emotions are apt to rule rather than clear logic which, in the long run, would benefit the veterans as well as the civilian population.

Certainly, as far as women were concerned, they did not get much help after World War I from the Veterans Preference Act. Instead, because of the mistaken zeal of a few ultrafeminists, they were deprived for a while of the opportunity that should have been theirs to hold jobs for which they were better qualified than veterans but for which they could not get a high enough rating on the civil service lists because the veterans came first.

Later on, during the depression, women again suffered much more than men. Even when they were on relief, women were the last to get employment and then only the tag ends, jobs with not very much pay. There was much criticism of the WPA and PWA for not doing more for women. Mrs. Ellen Woodward, head of the Women's Division of the WPA, set up all kinds of projects for women and, with her, we worked out certain standards for women's employment. We even tried to set up a liaison officer with Mrs. Woodward, but after one day she quit because she said there was nothing for her to do.

Mrs. Woodward was anxious to do more for women and, eventually, she accomplished a good deal but there was much criticism on the ground that women did not need relief and employment as much as men did.

Among all the discriminations against women, I think the agitation against the employment of married women is one of the most unjust and unsound. It is based on the false theory that all married women have someone to support them. That is a theory that we in the Women's Bureau have proved time and time again is not true.

More or less all through my life I have had to meet the question of whether or not married women should work for wages. The opposition to their employment always became very acute when there was a shortage of jobs. This was particularly true from 1929 on until World War II. The question came up all over the country and many state legislatures considered passing laws to prohibit married women from working. Some of the bills prohibited any employment of married women, not taking into consideration the fact that many of them would starve if they did not have a job. Other bills were introduced that prohibited more than one person in the family from working and some bills said that after eight hundred dollars came into the family during the year, no other person could be employed.

This agitation came about, of course, because of the very serious situation in the country — the lack of jobs due to the depression. I am glad to say that none of these state bills were passed but a law was passed by Congress at the very beginning of the depression, with the idea of spreading jobs so that only those who needed them could have them, stipulating that no two persons in any family could be employed in the government service. This superseded the previous regulation that no more than three persons in a family could work for the government. Although the new regulation applied to "persons" and not to women specifically, it worked out as a very great discrimination against women. If a man and his wife were both working for the government it was almost always the wife who had to give up her job because she was usually the one who got the least pay and it made more sense for the one who was earning the least to give up the job.

This regulation broke up families all over the city. Some husbands and wives separated and lived apart so that they would not be considered one family. We had one case in the Women's Bureau that was typical. The wife was a statistical clerk and her husband was a letter carrier. They were each earning less than two thousand dollars a year. They had two children and were buying a house. They were able to employ a good person to look out for the children and were getting along very well when this regulation went into effect. Then the wife had to give up her job. They could not keep up payments on their house unless she was working too, so eventually she had to go into the open market to get a job that was not under the government. She had the inconvenience of changing jobs and we lost a valuable worker from our staff.

There was a great deal of agitation about this regulation, especially from women's organizations such as the Business and Professional Women's clubs and the League of Women Voters. In the Women's Bureau we made an investigation of its effects and reported to Congress as well as to the Civil Service Commission. It took a number of years to get it repealed. I think one of the chief difficulties was the determination of Representative John J. Cochran of Missouri, who had sponsored the regulation, that married women should not be employed in the government, or anywhere else for that matter. Although ostensibly the regulation was not directed against women, in effect it worked against them. This was what he wanted and he was very stubborn to deal with.

The whole problem of the employment of married women is not easy to solve from the woman's standpoint or from the employer's standpoint either. All government employees have the right to accumulate sick and vacation leave with pay. The married woman in the government service can get sick leave with pay whenever she has a child and she can be sure of getting her job back when she returns. There are no such mandatory laws for private industry and I think if there were they would work against women. A married woman could be quite a liability to her employer and such a law might result in curtailed opportunities for women. I think the whole thing could be taken care of if the provider for the family got sufficient wages. Then married women would not be obliged to go to work to supplement an inadequate income for their families and could make their own choice as to what they should do.

Of course, during the war emergency, there was a real necessity for married women to take jobs and then certain things had to be done to make it possible for them to work. But I am not sure that the measures taken were really of very great assistance to them. No matter what services were set up for working mothers, shopping services, day nurseries, and the like, the fact always remained that they had to do their work at home and look after the children when they were not in the factory. In the morning the children had to be bathed, fed, and taken to the nursery. After the day's work in the factory was over the mother had to go back to the nursery to fetch the children, do the marketing and cooking, feed the children, and do the washing and all the other household chores. If a child was not well it could not be taken to the nursery and the mother had to stay away from the factory to take care of it.

I know there are those who will say that the child is better cared for at the nursery than at home and that may be true, but the wear and tear on the mother is something to be thought of too. She cannot be a very good mother if she is so tired she is ready to drop. As a social philosophy I think that the establishment of day nurseries for the children of working mothers is only a stopgap, not a solution of anything. In time of emergency it may be necessary but I would not want to see it a general custom. Married women should be free to make their own choice as to whether or not they should be employed outside of the home. But they should not be forced by economic necessity to take on the two jobs of homemaker and wage earner, each of which is a full-time occupation.

19

The So-Called Equal Rights Amendment

TALKING about discriminations against women naturally leads to the subject of the so-called equal rights amendment to the Constitution about which there has been so much controversy during the past twenty-five years.

This proposal to remove all discriminations against women through a constitutional amendment saying "Men and women shall have equal rights throughout the United States and every place subject to its jurisdiction," came up first in 1921 after the passage of the suffrage amendment. One of the organizations that had worked for the suffrage amendment was the Women's Congressional Committee of which Alice Paul was the head. The members of this committee were very ardent feminists and in working for the suffrage amendment had used sensational tactics, such as chaining themselves to the White House fence, burning effigies of President Wilson, and getting themselves sent to jail for violating the law in one way or another. Alice Paul herself had worked with the English "suffragettes" and was one of those who had been "jailed for freedom."

When the suffrage fight was won this group did not want to disband and they would not join with the new organization, the League of Women Voters, which was started by many members of the Woman Suffrage Association. They did not

know what program to propose for themselves, so they had
a meeting at the Belasco theater in Washington at which
almost every organization working for women was represented. They wanted to canvass what was being done for
women and find out what they could do that would be different. There were many speeches but no definite decisions
were made.

Many members of the International League for Peace and
Freedom were members of the Women's Congressional Committee and they urged Miss Paul to get out and work for
peace. Since she was a Quaker, they thought that would
appeal to her, but I guess she was more of a feminist than she
was a Quaker and she would not do that. Instead, the idea
of a constitutional amendment was developed. Women had
been successful in getting suffrage through a constitutional
amendment and this group now wanted to right every wrong
in the same way. So eventually the Women's Congressional
Committee became the National Woman's party and they
set out on their campaign. They did not seem to realize the
difference between the suffrage amendment, which granted
to women one specific right, and a general amendment such
as they proposed, which was really nothing more than a good
slogan.

After studying this proposed amendment for a time almost
all the national organizations of women were opposed to it.
We called it the "blanket amendment" because that was what
it was and we knew it was not the way to get the kind of
equality for women that we wanted. We really tried very
hard at first to work with the National Woman's party and
find a wording for the proposed amendment that would really
accomplish something. The National Women's Trade Union
League, the Consumers League, the newly organized League
of Women Voters, the General Federation of Women's
Clubs, and the National Council of Catholic Women took
the amendment very seriously from the very first. We consulted eminent lawyers, asking them what they thought the

effect of the amendment would be and if they could suggest a wording that would be more certain to accomplish what we wanted. I think Ethel Smith of the National Women's Trade Union League was one of the most active persons in trying to get at the real facts of the situation.

After months of consultation with every authority we could think of we finally decided that we could not go along with the Woman's party in this matter. The amendment which they suggested was so vague and covered such a tremendous field there was no telling what its effect would be. The only sure thing was that if this amendment was adopted it would throw into the courts every law affecting men and women in every state. Inheritance, property ownership, divorce, social security, mothers' pensions — every law that was not identical for men and women could be considered "unequal" and would have to be made the same, either the men's standard adopted for the women or the women's standard for the men, as the courts would decide.

Then there was the question of differences in the state laws. The amendment said, "Men and women shall have equal rights throughout the United States and every place subject to its jurisdiction." Did that mean that the women in Florida should have the same rights as the men in Maine? What would such a phrase in the Constitution do to state rights? There was no answer.

Finally, and to us perhaps the most important question of all, what would the amendment do to all the labor legislation that applied to women?

When Alice Paul first showed me the proposed amendment I raised that question immediately. I said I was afraid it might hurt labor legislation and she replied, "If we find that it will hurt labor legislation will you propose some wording that will obviate that?"

A few weeks later she came to me and said, "You haven't given me the wording I asked for." My answer was that the amendment could not be worded so as to safeguard labor legislation; that if it was adopted there was no doubt that it would do away with all special legislation for women in every state. "It won't do anything of the kind!" was her reply and she was so furious with me that she would not speak to me for a long time afterward.

Then the proponents of the amendment tried to persuade the National Women's Trade Union League to go along with them, saying that the amendment would not affect labor legislation for women. Mrs. Robins, Elisabeth Christman, and Ethel Smith had a long conference with Maud Younger, who was then working for the amendment but who had been instrumental in getting the eight-hour law for women in California. She had done so much that the waitresses in California gave her an honorary membership in their union in recognition of her services. She declared that the amendment would not hurt labor legislation and said, "You don't think I would want that, do you, after what I did in California?"

In the end, when they found they could not get any of the other women's organizations to go along with them on their say-so, and in spite of all the expert advice we had had to the contrary, that labor legislation for women would not be affected, the Woman's party reversed its attitude and said that the amendment would wipe out special legislation for women and that that was what they wanted to do because special legislation was a handicap to women and limited their opportunities. Then the fat was really in the fire and the battle began that was to go on for twenty-five years and is not entirely settled yet.

The trouble with the whole thing was that they had coined a phrase that was hard to beat. No one is against "equal rights" for women and that phrase is the most powerful argument they have. When it was presented to them congressmen and senators did not have the time to go into the question very minutely. They gave their support when they were asked "You're for equal rights for women, aren't you?" None of them would say No to that question and then the first thing they knew they were quoted as being in favor of the amendment. The phrase put all the people who were working seriously for the advancement of women in a very awkward position. We had to take a stand in opposition to the amendment because we knew that it would do a great deal of harm and would accomplish nothing that could not be accomplished more surely by other means. But the proponents of the amendment, led by the National Woman's party, were past masters in the art of getting publicity and would not be hampered by a consideration of the facts. They appealed to prejudice and hysteria and, through the years, they made considerable headway because it is always easier for people to adopt a slogan that sounds fine than to face facts and get the remedies little by little.

No one knew better than we did that there were many legal discriminations against women on the statute books of the various states. We were working to get these discriminations removed and we were making headway. But we were certain that the so-called equal rights amendment to the Constitution would not do the job. In the first place it was unsound from the legal point of view. There was no definition of "rights." There was no definition of "equality." If a state law had different standards for men and women, would the amendment mean that the men should have the women's standards, or the women have the men's? No one knew the answer. In the second place it was unnecessary because most of the real discriminations against women were a matter of custom and prejudice and would not be affected by a constitutional amendment. In the third place it was dangerous because it might upset or nullify all the legal protection for women workers that had been built up through the years, which really put them on a more nearly equal footing with men workers.

It was on this last subject — labor legislation for women — that the most bitter controversy raged. The record shows that at the beginning the proponents of the amendment took the position that it would not nullify labor legislation for women and that they wanted to avoid any possibility of this by getting a wording that would satisfy us. When they found that they could not get us to go along, they reversed their position and opposed labor legislation for women, claiming that it hampered women's opportunities if there were laws setting standards for their employment.

I think it was in 1921 that we had the first congressional hearing on the amendment. After that at intervals of two or three years there were hearings whenever the Woman's party could bring enough pressure to bear on the members of the House or Senate Judiciary committees. The hearings were always about the same. After the first hearings all the organizations opposing the Woman's party felt very resentful of what we considered a waste of our time and a waste of the time of the members of Congress, just to provide a forum for the Woman's party. They would always produce some so-called "working woman" who would rave and rant about the injustices she had suffered because of labor legislation. On our side the opposing organizations were united in a committee with a chairman for the hearing and under her leadership we would present bona fide representatives of the trade union movement telling of their opposition to the amendment, but it was usually the most sensational speakers who got the publicity and that was all the Woman's party wanted.

I remember one hearing that was quite a lot of fun for us. We decided not to give them a chance to put on their usual act. As was customary, each side was given a certain amount of time for its testimony. Part of the time was used for presenting the arguments and part for rebuttal. We had an understanding with the committee that any time our side did not use would not be given to the proponents.

The Woman's party had the first inning and as usual saved most of their time for rebuttal, hoping to make the headlines by attacking our speakers. When our time came the chairman of our group did not present any speakers. She referred to the great pile of testimony given in previous hearings, presented the documents of these hearings, and then filed a great sheaf of statements signed by all the organizations that were in opposition to the amendment. Then she said that she did not think it was necessary to take up the time of the committee presenting additional statements on a subject that had already been so fully discussed. That was the end of our testimony. The committee was grateful to have it over so quickly and the Woman's party was out on a limb — they had a lot of time left but they did not have any speakers to rebut and they could not have their usual forum.

In the early days of this controversy we used to treat the Woman's party seriously and meet them in debates and try to show through the facts how dangerous their proposition was. But after a while we found it was not worth doing. We could not meet their hysterical prejudices with any facts that would get their attention, so we gave it up.

One of our most serious attempts to work with them came in 1926 after the Women's Bureau held the Second Women's Industrial Conference in Washington.

I called this conference to stimulate action for better standards for women in industry. When the news of the conference first got out certain women from the Republican organization, aided and abetted by members of the Woman's party, went to the secretary of labor, James J. Davis, and said that I should not be allowed to have the conference because I was not loyal to the Republican party. The secretary replied that this was not a question of party politics, that there was no danger of anyone's being disloyal to the Constitution and the institutions of the United States, and that he would uphold me in calling the conference.

It was a good meeting. We had a splendid program on standards and methods of enforcing them, with able and responsible people to lead the discussion. In all, we had 291 delegates representing 107 national organizations and 41 states, the District of Columbia, Puerto Rico, and the Philippines. We included the National Woman's party in our invitation to send delegates but at first they refused to send anyone unless we put the equal rights amendment on the program. This, of course, we would not do. The conference was called to discuss specific standards for women in industry and we could not open it to discussion of the special programs of the 107 national organizations that were sending delegates. If we opened it to one we would have to open it to all, and we would get nowhere. Finally, after much correspondence, the Woman's party decided to send delegates. We found out later that their plan was to stampede the conference. They tried their best to do this but they did not succeed.

When we started the afternoon session on the second day, I opened the meeting and was about to introduce the woman who would preside when the Woman's party delegates and many of their friends who had come with them got up on the floor and started an uproar by all shouting and speaking at the same time. As well as we could gather through the noise they were making, what they wanted us to do was to set aside the program for the afternoon and discuss the equal rights amendment. Of course, we would not do that. Our speakers, including one from the National Manufacturers Association, were on the platform. It was no time to consider setting the program aside. The members of the Woman's party knew this and did not even give us a chance to consider their motion. For fully an hour they kept up an uproar so loud that you could not hear yourself think. They rushed up and down the aisles shouting and haranguing and making as much commotion as they could.

There was nothing we could do. I could not get order so I just let them go on. I remember distinctly one woman who was a delegate from Pittsburgh. She was a big, powerful person and was standing at the back of the hall near the entrance. All at once she walked up the aisle to the speakers' platform and called up to me, "Mary, if you want me to put them out, I'll put them out." But I said No, because I knew that was just what they wanted. Some of the younger women in the Women's Bureau were serving as ushers and they got very excited and wanted to send for the police. But we knew that was the one thing the Woman's party wanted most, the newspaper headlines would be really sensational; we kept the entrance doors closed and let the tumult rage. It really was funny to see them shrieking and stamping in the aisles, just like children having tantrums. At one moment, Mary Mc-Dowell, who was sitting in the front row, called up to me, above the noise, "Never mind, Mary, anyway you have on a fine-looking hat!"

Finally, Mrs. Ella Boole, president of the Women's Christian Temperance Union, who was to be the presiding officer, took the gavel. She was a large woman with a booming voice. The demonstrators were getting tired by that time, she got order, and we went on with our program.

That evening a few of us met together and decided that it might be a good thing to have a discussion of the amendment so that the delegates would know what it was all about. This meeting was not to be part of the regular program of the conference, but instead would be a special meeting on the one subject. We had speakers pro and con and Mrs. Boole was the chairman. It was a fiery meeting. The Woman's party members spoke first and then they alternated with the opposition. I will never forget Melinda Scott when she spoke. She was the hatmaker from England who had so disturbed Andrew Furuseth at an American Federation of Labor convention. Very small and very belligerent in her opposition, she tramped up and down the platform saying, "If anyone wants a licking I'm here to lick 'em!" The last speaker of the evening was Doris Stevens, representing the Woman's party. She spoke against night-work laws for women. Her concluding remark was that men were back of the laws prohibiting women from working at night because they wanted their women at home in the conjugal bed! The meeting ended on that note and we realized that what we were up against was not a serious attempt to get at the real problems of women, but instead a kind of hysterical feminism with a slogan for a program.

In the years to come we were to learn how difficult it is to combat that kind of campaign. Facts seemed to have little influence. Propaganda and prejudice and confusion were more effective.

As a result of that meeting at the Second Women's Industrial Conference, the Women's Bureau was requested to make a study of the effects of labor legislation on opportunities for women. We accepted that request in good faith. It seemed to me that this was a question on which we really should have the facts. It was possible that in some cases the allegations made by the Woman's party had some foundation. No one had seriously examined all the effects of the special laws for women that had been put on the statute books. I felt that the time was ripe for such a study and we took on the job with much interest. Our aim was to make it an absolutely objective investigation and to get the facts with a completely unprejudiced mind.

So that both sides would be satisfied with the findings, I appointed a consulting committee to advise about the general policies to be followed in the investigation. On this committee were three members of the Woman's party, Alice Paul, Doris Stevens, and Maud Younger. To represent the other side I appointed Sarah Conboy of the American Federation of Labor, Mabel Leslie of the National Women's Trade Union League, and Maud Wood Park of the League of Women Voters. To help us in the very difficult technical problems that I knew would arise in an investigation of this sort, I appointed a technical committee consisting of Mary van Kleeck, then of the Russell Sage Foundation, who was a specialist in making social investigations, Dr. Charles P. Neill, who as assistant commissioner of labor had directed the great investigation of women and child wage earners, and Mrs. Lillian Gilbreth, who was a well-known engineer as well as the mother of eleven children. Mary Winslow was appointed to direct the entire investigation and to prepare the report.

At the very first meeting of the consulting committee we ran into a snag with the members of the Woman's party. They did not want a regular fact-finding, technical investigation. Instead, they insisted we should get our facts by holding open hearings. We knew that by holding such forums we would get just opinions and not real facts; we felt that the only useful thing we could do was to make a scientific investigation, using the techniques we had already developed in the Women's Bureau for collecting accurate information. We discussed this back and forth, if you could call it discussion, and got nowhere. Then we had a second meeting and again came to no decision.

In the meantime, the Woman's party was working on members of Congress, getting them to tell us that we should hold open hearings. I began to get letters and telephone messages to this effect. I felt that we could not go on that way and that the members of the Woman's party who were on our consulting committee were behaving in a very unethical way. Holding a public forum for discussion would not be an investigation and the Women's Bureau could not be party to such an undertaking. I did not know just what to do. It is difficult for a government official to "buck" demands from members of Congress, but I was not willing to compromise the standards of the Women's Bureau. Fortunately, the decision was taken out of my hands by the other members of the consulting committee who felt as I did. They declined to go along any further on a committee with the Woman's party because they felt that they could not work with them. They sent me a telegram in which they outlined the kind of fact-finding investigation they wanted, said that there was no point in meeting with the members of the Woman's party any longer because they were too busy to spend their time in wrangling, and resigned from the consulting committee. Copies of this telegram were sent to the newspapers and by the time I received it, the *Washington Post* had it on the front page.

That action simplified my problem. I had tried to have a bipartisan consulting committee, but because the members representing one side had all resigned, the committee was no longer bipartisan and it was dissolved. Then we went on with the investigation, with the help of the technical committee.

The investigation started out in a small way but it ended by being a very extensive and expensive proposition. When we started we knew it would be important but we did not realize it would end up by using almost the entire staff and nearly the whole appropriation of the Women's Bureau for about two years.

When the facts were all in we found that the claims that women were prevented from getting jobs or lost their jobs because of labor legislation could not be substantiated. We found that women lost their jobs for every kind of reason, just as men do, but not because of any legislation regarding hours and wages.

I remember one woman whose record was typical of many others. She was a station agent, working in New England, and there was a lot of excitement about her because it was said that she had lost her job when a law limiting women's hours to nine a day had gone into effect. When our agents studied the situation they found that the law did not apply to employees of railroads and she got her job back in a day or two. We did find that laws had to be carefully drafted so that they would not set up impossible standards for certain occupations where the work was continuous, such as street railways and subways, or where the shifts had to be interrupted, as in restaurants. We also found in a few instances that certain occupations were prohibited for women for no conceivable reason except prejudice. In such cases our position was, as it had been in our earliest investigations in the war industries of Niagara Falls, that it was the job that should be regulated and not the women.

On the whole, however, our survey of the facts of women's employment in eleven states in more than twelve hundred factories employing more than six hundred thousand persons showed that labor legislation was not a handicap to women, that it did not reduce their opportunities, and that it raised standards not only for women but for thousands of men too.

We got a tremendous amount of publicity from this report. It was generally accepted as accurate and sound and was used all over the country but it did not stop the agitation against labor laws for women. The Woman's party still attacked the investigation, saying it should have been made through public hearings. They usually ignored the facts we had accumulated with so much care and when they had to mention the facts they misstated them. Even now they still talk about the women on the subways in New York, saying that they lost their jobs because of legislation, although we spent months getting information about this situation and found that the real reason they lost their jobs was that the companies wanted to take back the men who had returned from war service.

In spite of everything we could say and do about the dangers of the equal rights amendment, we were not able to convince the members of the National Woman's party. Their agitation has gone on ever since and their slogan has been so appealing that they have made considerable progress. We have felt very bitter about the way they have impeded the passage of special legislation for women. Time and time again they have tried to defeat proposed legislation, not openly, but by saying that they wanted it to apply to both men and women, knowing all the time that it would not be possible or even constitutional to include men in the law. We were convinced that in some cases the Woman's party was used as a front by the employers' associations that wanted to kill legislation for women.

Year after year organizations such as the National Women's Trade Union League, the League of Women Voters, the National Consumers League, and many others had to lay aside the work they were doing to improve conditions for women and spend their time combating the equal rights amendment. Members of the Woman's party developed a powerful lobby in Congress and with the political parties. Their nuisance value became so great that many members of Congress agreed to bring the amendment up for a vote, in order to get rid of it. Other members of Congress, confused by the slogan, thought it was what women wanted and did not dare to come out against "equal rights" for women.

The issue was taken into the international field and here again it was confused, this time with the right to vote. We had to be on guard everywhere to see that the issue was clarified and that, through international agreements, the principle of special legislation for women should be upheld and the specific rights, such as the right to vote, should be endorsed. We were successful in doing this in the conferences of the League of Nations and the International Labor Organization, and in the Pan-American conferences, but it has not been an easy task and much animosity has developed among women's organizations in consequence. It has been a most unfortunate and time-consuming controversy and has held up other far more important projects for the improvement of the status of women. After twenty-five years of it I must confess I am tired of it and hope that in the near future it will be settled once for all, so that we can turn our attention to something more constructive than a slogan.

20

Presidents and Secretaries of Labor

ALL during those early years in the Women's Bureau I had my own personal problems to solve as well as those of the bureau. When the change came from the Wilson to the Harding administration, I felt that I was very much "on the spot." My name went up to the Senate for confirmation, but because the Republican Senate was not approving Wilson appointees, my job terminated on March 4. Then there was the question of my reappointment and a whole month elapsed after March 4 until the reappointment took place. It was an anxious time for me because I knew I was not a political asset to either of the major parties. I had never contributed to either party and it was just because of sheer good will on the part of a number of women in the Republican party that I was reappointed.

Mrs. Harriet Taylor Upton was then head of the Women's Committee of the National Republican Committee. I had known her slightly before she came to Washington and she became a great friend of mine. She said that she would urge the President to reappoint me. There was also a tremendous amount of work done by the women throughout the country on this reappointment, the National Women's Trade Union League taking a leading part in organizing support. There were literally thousands of letters sent to the secretary of labor urging my appointment.

The matter came to a head one day when the Republican Women's Committee was meeting with the President at the White House. Mrs. Upton had told me she was going to bring up my appointment that day. In the meantime, a member of our staff who knew Mrs. Douglas Robinson very well was able to see her and tell her how important it was that I should be reappointed. Mrs. Robinson was a sister of Theodore Roosevelt, the former President, and was a member of the Republican Women's Committee. At that time she was very provoked at the President because he had not appointed her nephew, Theodore Roosevelt, Jr., to any position. In the midst of the conversation the committee were having with the President, Mrs. Robinson suddenly burst out and said, "And when are you going to reappoint Mary Anderson?" The President replied, "I am going to in a few days, just as soon as I get to it." Mrs. Upton said that she was completely astonished, but they all supported Mrs. Robinson and the President appointed me as he had said he would.

After that, the question of my appointment did not come up again. The precedent had been established that my position was nonpolitical and with the aid of the women's organizations it remained so. I held my job under five Presidents, two Democrats and three Republicans. I always voted for the man I thought would do the most good and was the most liberal. As it turned out, I always voted for the Democratic presidential candidates, but not for the straight Democratic ticket.

Although the question of my reappointment did not come up again, there were a few times when I wondered if I was going to have to resign. Sometime during the Coolidge administration, a story went around Washington that Grace Abbott, chief of the Children's Bureau, and I were not loyal to the administration and that we should resign. One day I was called over to the Department of Labor by the chief clerk, who said that the secretary felt that I was embarrassing the President and ought to resign. I said to him, "If the secretary feels that way about me I would certainly like to hear it from his own lips. He will have to tell me himself." The reply was, "Why don't you go over to see him?"

I went back to my office and thought it over and decided that if I went to see him he would probably ask me for my resignation; I thought it would be better to wait until he sent for me.

In the meantime, Elisabeth Christman wrote to Raymond Robins, who was an adviser to the President. He came immediately to Washington and I talked to him. That evening he had dinner at the White House and, during a long talk with the President, brought up the question of Grace Abbott and me. The President said, "I know of no embarrassment they are causing me and there won't be any danger that they will be asked to resign." We heard nothing more about "disloyalty" after that.

When Mr. Hoover was elected, I knew him personally. I had been at the Hoovers' home a number of times and he had said to others, Mr. and Mrs. Robins particularly, that he thought I had done good work. The first time I ever met Mr. Hoover was at a meeting of a committee that was set up after World War I to find out about the living and working conditions of people both in the United States and in Europe. Miss Lathrop, then the chief of the Children's Bureau, was asked to testify in regard to children and I was asked to testify in regard to women.

Mr. Hoover was not always at the meetings, but the evening I testified he was there. At that time I had a great deal of information about the women in Italy and the peasant women in some of the other countries. I had kept up a correspondence with Mme. Casertelli of Italy and many other delegates whom I had met at international conferences. Also, when I was in Paris during the Peace Conference I had had a long talk with one of the members of the Italian delegation about the conditions of women in Italy. As a result I had a good deal of information to give to the committee that evening.

Mr. Hoover was particularly interested and said, "I didn't know anything about women's conditions in Italy, but I have had more information on this subject this evening than I have ever had before."

Later I was invited to have dinner with the Hoovers and we talked a great deal about general conditions for women. Mrs. Hoover was, at that time, very much interested in the women's organizations in this country. She presided many times at meetings that I attended and I always felt that she was very liberal and understanding.

When Mr. Hoover took over the presidency, I happened to be in Florida visiting for a few days with Mr. and Mrs. Robins. On my return I was told that I must send in my resignation. I eventually did this, submitting it through Secretary of Labor Davis one morning. When I got back from lunch that afternoon, there was one of the biggest rose bushes I have ever seen standing in my office and a letter from Mr. Hoover asking me to stay on. It was a fine letter and I still have a copy of it. It said:

My dear Miss Anderson:

I wish to thank you for the courtesy you have shown me in tendering your resignation as Director of the Women's Bureau of the Department of Labor. I am returning it to you without acceptance as I am anxious that you should continue the distinguished service you have been giving there.

Yours faithfully,

Herbert Hoover

In looking at my letter of resignation, which was enclosed, I was interested to see a penciled memorandum that had not been completely erased. It gave me an idea of what I owed my reappointment to, for it said, "Miss Anderson desires to remain. Raymond Robins, Women's Trade Union League, AF of L and others recommend"!

I had know the Roosevelts for a long time before they came to Washington. I also knew the people who had been running the campaign and I did not think there was any question about keeping me on the job. I had met the Roosevelts through the Women's Trade Union League in New York. Mrs. Roosevelt always came to the meetings and was very active in the league for many years. Before Mr. Roosevelt became governor of New York the league was invited to a picnic at Hyde Park. I was in New York at the time and went with them. We had a perfectly wonderful time. Mr. Roosevelt stayed with us at the picnic almost the whole afternoon.

I also had had many conferences with him when he was assistant secretary of the navy and I was first in the Woman in Industry Service. He always received us very cordially and tried to correct the conditions we brought to his attention. Once we discovered that the women in the naval storage plants were working under very bad conditions. Women were new to this kind of work, which had previously been done by men who accepted the bad conditions without protest. We went to Mr. Roosevelt and told him and his secretary, Louis Howe, of the situation; it was immediately remedied at his suggestion.

Another time we went to Mr. Roosevelt about the women flagmakers who were working in a loft under bad conditions as well as low wages. Again the situation was improved without much delay. We were always hopeful when we went to him with problems of this sort and had real confidence in his interest and willingness to act. In those days I thought he was the most handsome man I had ever seen, tall and erect, with his famous smile and engaging manner. I did not know Mrs. Roosevelt at that time, but I felt I knew him very well.

I remember a luncheon I went to a couple of weeks after they came to the White House in 1932. Louis Howe, who was sitting just across the table from me, leaned over and said, "I knew you in the Navy Department. You used to come there with all kinds of troubles," and I replied, "I remember too, and we were always courteously received and you always did what we asked you to do."

It happened to be Army Day and someone asked, "Where is the parade going to be?" President Roosevelt answered, "I don't know," and he leaned over and asked me. I said, "I don't know, but I think it will be on Constitution Avenue." Then he asked, "Where is Constitution Avenue?" and I told him, "It's the old B Street." But that was not enough for him and he asked, "Where was B Street?" I explained, "It was along by the foot of 17th Street down by the Navy Department," and he said, "Oh, we used to call that the old white lot!"

On the whole I think I was very fortunate in the relations I had with the five Presidents I served under. Of course, during the years of the Roosevelt administration I felt much closer to the White House because of Mrs. Roosevelt's interest and friendship. She always knew what we were doing and understood what our problems were. I felt that working women everywhere could turn to her for help and support, and through her could get the kind of sympathetic interest from the President that would be very helpful.

But, of course, my actual contacts with the White House were very limited. It was my relationship with the various secretaries of labor that presented a greater problem.

When the Woman in Industry Service was first established the secretary of labor was William B. Wilson, a fine labor man with whom I had very friendly contacts but, because Mary van Kleeck was the director of the service, she was the person who dealt directly with the secretary and I had very few meetings with him.

My first real tussle with a secretary of labor occurred when James J. Davis came in. Shortly after I was appointed director of the Women's Bureau Senator Harry S. New from Indiana urged the secretary to insist that I appoint a woman from Indianapolis as an assistant. He wanted a three-thousand-dollar job for her. She came to me and I asked her what she knew about women in industry. She said she didn't know a thing about them. I then asked how she expected to do the job and she said she didn't know but she wanted the three thousand dollars. I replied that we had no job for her and then she asked what I was going to do about it. I said, "Do you know what I have to do in order to appoint you or anyone else outside of civil service? I have to tell the civil service that you have special qualifications for doing a special job that I can't get anyone from the civil service register to do. I can't do that because you have said you know nothing. I have no special funds to pay you for the job and I'm not going to tell the civil service something that isn't true."

Later on I had a telephone call from a friend who was the Republican committeewoman from Indiana. She said, "If you employ that woman, we will never trust anything that comes out of the Women's Bureau." She said the women in Indiana did not trust her and could not have anyone like that in the Women's Bureau. I said, "Well, the answer is that I can't employ her."

When the secretary found out about my talk with the woman who wanted the job he sent for me. Before I went to his office I wrote out my resignation and put it in my pocket. He started out with a question: "You're not going to appoint Miss ———?" I answered, "Have you any money to pay her with?" He said No and I said I did not have any either. I told him then about the telephoned protest and he agreed that I was right and directed me to let it go.

He did not seem to bear me any ill will for not making the appointment, for later on he asked me if I would organize women in an auxiliary to the Loyal Order of Moose, in which he was very prominent. The salary, he suggested, would be ten thousand dollars, or "anything I wanted." I refused his offer, saying that I did not know anything about fraternal organizations and that I did not believe in organizing women into auxiliaries but thought they should take the same part that men did. After I turned down the job, he gave it to the woman from Indiana who had wanted to be my assistant!

Later on I almost got into trouble with Secretary Davis
when we made a study of the conditions of working women
in Ohio, where there were going to be hearings on an eight-
hour law for women in that state. We rushed out some advance information about the conditions we had found during
our investigation. I sent a copy of this material to the assistant
secretary of labor, Edward J. Henning, who had said he
wanted to see it before we issued it because it was about conditions in President Harding's home state. Henning looked
over our report and sent me a memorandum saying that it
was an excellent job. I then sent copies to the Ohio Consumers League and to the Ohio Manufacturers Association. Unfortunately, there was another employers' association in Ohio
that we did not know anything about and did not send a copy
of our report to. When its executive secretary came to the
legislative hearing and heard the testimony of our findings
he was furious. He was a special friend of the President,
so he hopped on a train and came right to Washington.

In the meantime, we had sent a release about our findings
to the newspapers. When the man from Ohio got to Washington, he saw Mr. Henning, who sent word that I must recall our release to the newspapers. I knew that we could not
do that without stirring up a tremendous row, so I went to
Mrs. Upton for advice. She said, "Don't do anything about
it. You can't unscramble scrambled eggs!"

The next day I went to see Secretary Davis in his office,
taking my resignation with me for a second time. He knew
nothing about the matter because it had all been handled by
Mr. Henning, but when I explained that I had Mr. Henning's
memorandum saying the report was excellent and asked what
he thought the newspapers would do to the Women's Bureau
and the Department of Labor if we tried to recall the report
we had issued, he agreed with me and said, "No, we can't do
that. But Henning is very angry with you." While I was with
the secretary, Henning came into the office and looked dag-
gers at me, but I did not give in. We did not withdraw the

report or repudiate the findings and eventually Henning and I buried the hatchet.

On the whole I got on very well with Secretary Davis, although I felt that in spite of the fact that he had been a puddler and knew what hard work and poor living conditions meant, he always had a very sentimental approach to the problems of women in industry and to general economic problems too. At that time there was much talk about "normalcy" and I remember one day he said to me, "What we really need in this country is to get back to the good old times." When I asked how far back he thought we should go, he said, "When I was a puddler in a mill I was very happy. I made four dollars a day." I said, "I was working in a shoe factory at that time and there were very few days when I earned as much as two dollars a day. I'd hate like fury to go back to those good old times."

One time while Mr. Davis was secretary of labor we were asked by the Consumers League of Kentucky to make a survey of the conditions of women workers in that state. I went to Kentucky to confer with various people and while I was there I called on the secretary of the Manufacturers Association and told him what we were going to do. When we finished the survey and published our findings, in which we reported that there were certain plants that had very poor standards of hours and working conditions, the secretary of the Manufacturers Association came to us asking for the names of those employers, saying he wanted to see that they improved the conditions in their plants.

I was pretty sure that his idea was to get their names so as to club them into his organization, telling them he would protect them if they joined. I refused to give the names, because our policy was always to keep our information confidential so far as individual employers were concerned, not to publish the conditions of individual firms, and never to take records from less than three firms in a given industry because we did not want them to be identified.

Finally, he came to Washington, went to the secretary of labor, and criticized everything he could about me personally. Surely the information was incorrect, he complained, or I wouldn't be afraid to give him the names; he had told the manufacturers so. He felt that Secretary Davis should get rid of a person like me because it was not good for the government to employ anyone who was so biased.

Mr. Davis said, "When you write me a letter to that effect, I'll take it up with Miss Anderson." A few days later when he had received the letter he sent for me and said, "What have you to say about it?" I told him of our policy not to give out names of employers included in our investigations and I said, "I am sure he wanted the names so that he could force them into the employers' association. I would not give him the names any more than I would give them to the trade unions or the business agents so that they could club the workers into the unions." Mr. Davis told me to write him a letter saying just that, which I did, and I never heard any more about it.

Eventually Secretary Davis quit and William Doak was appointed in his place. Doak was a railroad man and although I do not think he was an outstanding secretary, I always felt that personally he was very likable. I got well acquainted with him and worked with him a great deal. In fact, I think I had pleasanter personal relations with him than with any other secretary of labor, perhaps because he was the kind of labor man I was accustomed to working with and we spoke the same language. Anyway, he "went to town" for the Women's Bureau. One time when he was at home sick in bed we heard that the Bureau of the Budget had taken off ten thousand dollars from the Women's Bureau and twenty thousand dollars from the Children's Bureau appropriations. The chief of the Children's Bureau and I went to see the secretary at his home and told him about it. He said that if we would write a letter to President Hoover he would sign it. We heard that when the letter got to the President he called the director of the budget and said, "Put back that God-damned chicken feed," and it was put back!

I remember one time when I was able to give Mr. Doak some useful advice. He was having a newspaper fight with Donald Richberg, who was then attorney for the railroad unions. I happened to be walking by the Department of Labor building one morning just as the secretary stepped out of his car. When he saw me he said, "Come along up with me," so I accompanied him to his office where his secretary was much surprised to see me because we had come in unannounced through the private entrance.

The secretary told me he was planning to send a telegram in answer to some statement of Richberg's and was going to say that Richberg was getting an enormous fee, thirty thousand dollars, from the five big railroad organizations. I said, "Richberg has done good work, hasn't he?" and the secretary agreed. "Well," I went on, "if you split that amount up among five organizations, it isn't too much for any one of them." He thought that over for a while and then I asked, "Do you really have to send that telegram?" He answered, "No, by God, no!" He stuck his notes in a drawer and nothing ever came of it.

When Frances Perkins came in as secretary of labor, we were all jubilant, because we thought that at last we would have someone who really understood our problems and what we were up against and would fight for us. I felt that I had a friend to whom I could go freely and confidently, but it did not turn out to be that way. During the first months when she was secretary, I was truly sorry for her. She had so many difficult problems on her hands, because of the depression and the split in the labor movement. The terrible publicity she was subjected to because she was the first woman Cabinet officer was a great handicap. I wanted to do anything I could to help and with my contacts in the labor movement I hoped I could be of some use, but there never seemed to be anything I could do. It was especially discouraging to me to find that the Women's Bureau was not of great interest to her, though I understood that she was preoccupied with other things and did not want to be thought of as a woman who was too closely identified with women's problems.

In April 1933, just a few months after she had been made secretary, I got a real shock which seriously hampered me in my relationship with her during the years to come. Like every new secretary, when she first took office she did not know a great deal about government routine, appropriations, and so on, and, because she had great plans for the department, she wanted more freedom in handling the department appropriations that had been granted by Congress. She suggested to me that the appropriation for the Women's Bureau be turned over to her to be allocated in the way she felt would be most useful. I was appalled at this suggestion, because I felt it would establish a precedent that might eventually threaten the existence of the bureau. It had taken many years of effort on the part of women and women's organizations to establish a statutory bureau in the Labor Department to deal with women's problems. Miss Perkins assured me that the work of the bureau would not suffer under this arrangement and I am sure she meant it. But, if this arrangement was made, the bureau was in danger of losing its statutory position and its program would be entirely dependent on the good will of future secretaries of labor who might, or might not, be sympathetic to our work. I pointed out to Miss Perkins the danger of establishing such a precedent and the outcry that it would cause among the many groups who had worked for so long to establish the bureau. I also offered to allocate such funds as she might need for other purposes and to put the members of my staff at her disposal, but I strongly protested against any arrangement that would take from the bureau's control the appropriations that Congress had passed specifically for our program. Fortunately, nothing more came of this suggestion, but I must confess the memory of it made things difficult for me from then on.

There were many new people brought into the department who had very close contacts with the secretary and I gradually found that I did not have the entree to her that I had hoped to have. When our appropriations were discussed with the Bureau of the Budget and the Appropriations committees in Congress, we had very little help from the secretary's office. I understood the reason for this and realized that there were many more important projects to be considered and pressed for. But as the years went on I became more and more discouraged at the lack of backing I received. I felt that I was fighting a losing battle among all the politics and strife that went on in the department. Eventually I decided that there was nothing I could do about it and I would just go along doing the best I could and stop worrying. That is what I did, and although the bureau did not get the appropriations I had hoped for and there were many things we had to leave undone, we kept on the job and I think we did useful work that will be of lasting value.

21

Personnel Problems

ALL the positions in the Women's Bureau, except my own, were under the civil service and I always found that this was a great protection, but at the same time it was often a great handicap to efficient administration. As Miss Lathrop, chief of the Children's Bureau, used to say, civil service is terrible but it is better than no civil service. I always felt that if civil service was ever done away with, it would have defeated itself, because of all the red tape and formulas that have developed. However, in spite of the interminable delays required to apply the civil service formulas, eventually you do get fairly good people. There is no question but that civil service is necessary and important. Without it we would have to go back to the "spoils system" with politicians appointing the personnel of government, and we would be swamped with incompetents. When politicians called on me to supply a job for anyone, I always took the position that they knew we were under civil service and that they just wanted me to say so and thus relieve them of the responsibility. During the early days of the Women's Bureau I was bothered a good deal in this way, but not in later years.

There was only once that I had a really bad time and that was with Mr. Davis when he was the newly appointed secretary of labor. At the time when Harding became president,

Attorney General Harry M. Daugherty issued a violent blast at civil service, saying the law must be repealed, and that we must go back to free appointments. Mr. Davis said the same thing and told me I would never get appropriations to amount to anything until he could make appointments in the Women's Bureau. He had no appointments there except me. I had to argue with him strenuously to convince him that since the law put the staff of the Women's Bureau under civil service, there was nothing I could do about it.

I think the chief trouble I had with the civil service was the length of time it took to get a job classified so that it would fit into their formulas, and then the delay that was caused by all the investigation and examination that had to be made before anyone could be appointed. When a really important person was being considered it would take from two to six months to get an appointment through. This delay was not due to insufficient staff or money to do the work. The system was simply not flexible enough, and there was too much red tape.

One of the controversies we had for years with the civil service was about appointing people in the professional grade who did not qualify under the civil service formula that appointees in this grade should have a college degree. For our top field agents, who investigated working conditions in factories and dealt with working people, we needed people who had had personal experience with industry and workers. There were very few women with this kind of experience who were college graduates. I know I was much criticized in some labor circles for not having more "bona fide" labor women on my staff. But it took years of negotiation with the civil service before I could persuade them to accept experience in certain fields in place of the college degree that the civil service formula required.

Another handicap of civil service is that it is difficult to get rid of an employee who is not satisfactory. Once persons are definitely appointed under the civil service the only way you can get rid of them is to prefer and sustain charges against them or to abolish the positions they hold.

I remember one girl we had with a temporary appointment as a report writer. She was most unsatisfactory. She was slow and did not know how to write and although we tried our best to teach her, it did not work, and we felt we could not keep her. Since she only had a temporary appointment, we could get rid of her without preferring charges or abolishing her position. Therefore, before her probation period was up we notified her that we would not keep her. But she had joined the CIO Federal Employees Union and protested to them. They had a meeting and there was a good deal of talk and a number of protests, but we sat tight and said nothing. When her time was up she was entitled to two weeks' vacation with pay. Instead of taking it she said she did not want a vacation, but would keep on with the job. For two weeks she came in every day and sat at her desk and did nothing. When her two weeks' "vacation" was up we took her desk and gave it to someone else and stopped paying her. And that was the end of her! If she had had a permanent civil service appointment it would have been far more difficult to get rid of her.

Although the civil service investigated all our employees so that they knew almost everything about them except how many fillings they had in their teeth, I did not come under civil service, being a presidential appointee. I was a good target, therefore, for anyone who wanted to attack the standards and program of the Women's Bureau. My first experience with this kind of attack came a few years after I was made director of the Women's Bureau when the *Dearborn Independent*, in 1924, published an article attacking me and many other women and women's organizations.

The attack was based on the famous "spider web" chart that had been prepared and circulated by someone in the Chemical Warfare Service in the War Department. This chart purported to show how prominent people and organizations were all linked with "subversive" organizations that were trying to further "bolshevism." My name did not appear but many other persons prominent in the field of social and labor activities were included and the National Women's Trade Union League was one of the featured organizations. There was a great outcry against this chart and protests from all kinds of people. Finally, a committee made up of representatives of various women's organizations and headed by Mrs. Maud Wood Park, president of the newly organized League of Women Voters, went to the secretary of war, John W. Weeks, to protest against the distribution of the chart by the War Department through the Chemical Warfare Service. The secretary promised to stop its circulation and assured the committee that he had known nothing about it and that it had been done by two employees in the Chemical Warfare Service without authorization.

But, in the meantime, the *Dearborn Independent* had published its article and had also published the chart. The article was entitled "Are Women's Clubs 'Used' by Bolshevists?" It was a wholesale attack on practically every well-known women's organization in the United States and their leaders, accusing them of trying to further Soviet and "bolshevik" programs in the United States, especially by their endeavors to get federal legislation for assistance to mothers and children in the United States. The article singled me out as the director of the Women's Bureau in the United States Department of Labor who had "succeeded in having printed by the Government of the United States this program of Women's and Children's Work minus only its Soviet label."

I was furious about this attack on me and I said that I was going to sue the publishers, but after I got legal advice it seemed unwise for a public official to get into this kind of controversy, and I did not go any further. The next thing that happened was that the Manufacturers Association of Kentucky republished the *Dearborn Independent* article in an effort to discredit the Women's Bureau report of a survey of women's employment in that state. They did not get very far with that, though, because the women's organizations in Kentucky were much aroused and went to bat for us. They were splendid in their support, and because of their protests, the attack on us did not have much effect.

But once a statement like that has been made it keeps cropping up, and later on we heard that the Daughters of the American Revolution had set up a kind of black list for the use of the members of their organization, who were warned not to ask the people on the list to speak at meetings of the DAR. I left Washington by train one afternoon while they were having their convention in Washington. This was a yearly affair that we used to call the "Damned Annual Row." When I opened the evening paper I saw on the first page that Grace Abbott, chief of the Children's Bureau, and Mary Anderson were charged with being socialists and therefore subversive!

When I got back to Washington I saw Miss Abbott and told her I thought we should write a letter to Mrs. Alfred J. Brosseau, who was head of the DAR, and ask her to produce proof of her statement that we were subversive. Miss Abbott said, "I don't think we ought to bother with it," but I insisted, "That story is being printed in the public press. We are public servants and I think we have no right not to deny it. I am for asking the newspaper people to come in and talk about it." Grace Abbott did not want to do that, so finally, after debating with myself for some time, I wrote a letter to Mrs. Brosseau. Meanwhile she had left for England to be presented to the queen, which was quite a commentary on the woman who headed the Daughters of the American Revolution!

That letter was not answered until she got back from England. She denied that she had said I was subversive or that the DAR had taken any action in regard to a black list. A few weeks later there was a reception in the Pan-American Union one evening and Miss Abbott, Mrs. J. Borden Harriman, and I were there. Mrs. Harriman had also been branded as subversive. A friend of ours asked, "Have you ever met Mrs. Brosseau?" When she heard we had not she said, "Well, she is right here," and took us up and introduced us saying, "Here are the ladies you think are subversive." We were all most polite but Mrs. Brosseau was very flustered.

That kind of thing kept on for about ten years, until finally the Dies Committee was set up. By that time almost every liberal in the United States had been branded as social-istic or subversive and later as communistic. I felt I was in good company anyway.

During the latter part of the 1930s when the Dies Com-mittee was busy stigmatizing people as subversive with no basis of fact, without rhyme or reason, I was called one day by the newspapers, asking if I belonged to an organization named the Committee for Freedom and Democracy. I asked why they wanted to know and they said that Congressman Harry H. Mason had put into the *Congressional Record* a statement that I was subversive because I belonged to this organization. I said that I did not belong to it and did not even know the name until they had mentioned it. They said they were sorry to hear this because they had hoped I would make a statement. I answered, "Well, I'll give you a statement. What is wrong with freedom and democracy? I have always believed in both of them." Thus, my name went into the rec-ords of the Dies Committee as subversive.

Not long after, I was reported to the Dies Committee again, this time by Senator Kenneth McKellar, who included me and Senator George Norris in his list. When my name was presented this time the chairman of the committee wanted to know if it was Marian Anderson, who he understood was a great singer. Senator Henrik Shipstead and Senator Charles W. Tobey asked, "Isn't that the woman who was finally made head of the Women's Bureau in the Department of Labor?" They agreed that I was a very estimable woman and added that it seemed to them that the list of names was ridiculous.

One of the things that was most shocking to me was the

irresponsible way in which these people would include names in a list and try to blast the reputations of people they really did not know anything about. But I got some amusement out of it just the same. After Congressman Mason of Illinois had presented my name to the Dies Committee as a member of the Committee for Freedom and Democracy, a woman from Illinois who was assembling records of distinguished women, including Jane Addams and Julia Lathrop, to put in the archives of Rockford College asked me for records of my life and put them in the archives too. The story was carried in the Rockford newspapers. I assume that a congressman always knows what is printed in his local papers. Anyway, it was a very short time before Congressman Mason was to come up for re-election. He wrote me a letter of congratulation and said he was very glad to know of this honor I had received. He did not realize that I was the same person he had put into the records of the Dies Committee.

When I heard that Senator Shipstead and Senator Tobey had defended me before the Dies Committee, I wrote to them and thanked them. I also told them about Congressman Mason's letter.

22

Ventures in International Relations

NOW that I look back, it seems that one of the most interesting things that happened to me in the first ten or fifteen years I was in the Women's Bureau was the gradual extension of my contacts with women in other countries. When I went to Paris at the time of the Peace Conference, I met many French women who were active in the labor movement and in England I saw many more, some of them old acquaintances from the days in Chicago and Hull House. From then on I began to meet more and more women from other parts of the world. But it was not until the Third International Congress of Working Women was held in Vienna in 1923 that I had a real chance to see at first hand what was going on in a number of countries. It was at this time, too, that I returned to Sweden and saw my brothers and my old home after an absence of thirty-five years.

I was one of the delegates to the international congress, but instead of traveling with the other delegates, I went ahead with Tracy Copp, Mary van Kleeck, and Mary LaDame, going first to Bergen, Norway. We saw quite a bit of Norway and while we were there we were taken under the wing of Mrs. Betzy Kjelsberg, who was a great leader of the Norwegian women. She was an old friend of ours, having come to Washington for the First International Congress of Women.

I will never forget the luncheon she and her organization gave for Tracy Copp and me in Oslo. When she introduced me to the guests she said I was the director of the United States! Everyone was very apprehensive because our country had not joined the League of Nations or the International Labor Organization, and actually with tears in their eyes they begged us to do so. We told them we were in perfect sympathy with them but that there was nothing we could do about it. I guess they realized then that I was not the director of the United States after all!

From there we went to Stockholm where I saw my relatives for the first time since 1888. My mother and father had died many years before but two of my brothers were there to meet me at the train. As we pulled into the station I was standing by the window and they recognized me immediately, saying, "There she is." They looked very much the same to me, only a little older and fatter. Meeting them this time was a strain in the beginning. After we had talked a few minutes, there did not seem to be anything more to say because the time had been so long since we had seen each other that we could not start where we had left off. Anyway, Swedes do not talk much. I really had a much better time with my family when I went back to Sweden in 1931 because then we could carry on from our last meeting.

I had talked almost no Swedish since I had left Sweden, but after about two weeks I found that I understood everything and got along very well, except that I had quite a time finding a vocabulary for the more or less technical things I wanted to discuss. I did not know the right words because I had never heard them at home when I was young. I was asked to make speeches, but I never did. I could not have done it in Swedish and there was no point in speaking in English. The papers made quite a fuss about me. I was rather embarrassed when the *Dagens Nyheter* carried a story with the headline A SWEDISH PEASANT GIRL — AN AMERICAN GOVERNMENT OFFICIAL: "Miss Mary Anderson has back of her a very ro-

mantic history — not romantic in the sense of adventure and
experience, but in her development and achievement. Surely
it is not an ordinary career that has brought a little Swedish
peasant girl past the stages of the immigrant, the servant, the
factory worker, the trade union leader to a high position in
the Department of Labor of the United States of America."

My brothers and I made an expedition to the country where
we were all born and raised. We went to the old home and
I took some pictures. It seemed to me there had not been one
change in the house or the garden or the little pond or the
barns. Even some of the flowers were the same.

I did not have much time for anything except meeting my
relatives, but when we were in Stockholm Kirsten Hesselgren,
head of the Inspection Service of the Department of Labor
and also a member of the *Rystag*, invited me to her house. She
was very interesting in her conversation about her work in
factory inspection, and in the years to come she became one
of the most prominent of the women at the International Labor Organization conferences and in the League of Nations.

One day, when I was with my brothers at an outdoor mu-
seum in Stockholm, a woman came up to me and said, "I
wonder if you know my brother in California?" I said California was a big place, but asked who her brother was. She
told me his name and said he was president of a union. I did
know him! She had a letter in English from her young
nephew and was very anxious to know what he said so I read
the letter and translated it for her. She was very happy because I could tell her how they were situated and how well
they were. She had picked me out as an American because
of my horn-rimmed glasses.

When we left Sweden we met the other delegates to the
congress in Berlin. It was very depressing there because it was
during the time of the terrible inflation. The mark was decreas-
ing in value so fast that whenever we bought anything the
clerks had to call up the bank to find out what the mark was
worth. I remember we had several prominent German women

for dinner at the Continental Hotel, where we were staying. It was a most beautiful dinner, good food and well served. There were seven of us and the check was a little over two million marks. To us that was just a bit more than five dollars.

After three days in Berlin, we were glad to leave. We spent a few days in Prague, but did not like it much. The people we had hoped to see were away on vacation and the language was not one that we could understand. The morning we left the taxi driver charged us all the Czech money we had left — about two American dollars. We had to wait in the station for four hours because the train was late. When we finally got on board we were hungry and went straight to the dining car, only to find that we had no Czech money. The conductor said, "I'll take your ten-dollar Express check and cash it at the border." But when we got to the border, we found we had forgotten that the bank would be closed because it was Sunday. Then the conductor said he would keep the Express check and send the change on to us at the American Express office in Vienna. I gave him my official card to show who we were.

Several days later, we went into Vienna from Schoenbrun Castle where the conference was, and Mrs. Robins and I went into the Express office. I asked about my change and the man said, "Do you really think you'll ever get that?" I said I thought I would and I bought a paper and sat down to read. All of a sudden, Mrs. Robins came up and said, "Your man is here." And sure enough, there he was with the change. So my confidence in his honesty was justified.

I have already told of the unfortunate outcome of the Third International Congress of Women. It was a very turbulent and unhappy time for us all, but nevertheless we managed to have some pleasant experiences. I remember meeting Dorothy Thompson at that time. She was interested in our meetings and attended many of them and gave us a lovely dinner in her beautiful house.

I have a vivid recollection of our living quarters in the Park

Hotel. Tracy Copp and I had a room there which belonged to a prince, then away on vacation. It was a very big room with a balcony. We used to say that one of us would never stay alone in that room because it seemed so mysterious with all his things left around. Sometimes we ordered our dinner sent up and had it on the balcony while we listened to Viennese music from the many beer gardens across the way on the street.

When the unhappy conference in Vienna was over we went on to Paris for some sightseeing and then to England for a week before we sailed for home. It was a valuable experience, and although we were very sad about the failure of the Vienna conference, I felt that I had learned a great deal about the women in other countries and had made many new contacts that would be very useful in the years to come.

My next excursion to foreign lands was in 1928 when I went to a meeting of women's organizations held under the auspices of the Pan-Pacific Union in Honolulu. Anne Satterthwaite, who was secretary of the Pan-Pacific Union in Hawaii, visited the United States and came to me to ask if I would participate in such a conference. I was quite taken with the idea. She showed me a good many pictures and I wanted very much to see the beautiful blooming trees.

I knew very little about the women of that part of the world and it seemed to me the program showed that the meeting would be a very important one. I asked the secretary, James J. Davis, about it; he approved and I started off. Elisabeth Christman and Jo Coffin went with me as delegates from the National Women's Trade Union League, and Caroline Manning, who was a field agent in the Women's Bureau, came along to make a survey of the conditions for women in the canning industry.

It was a beautiful trip. The ocean was smooth and warm and beautiful. The last day, however, I awakened with a fever which lasted almost all day and I was very sick. I don't know yet what it was, but probably it was the aftermath of over-fatigue in San Francisco, where I had spoken at so many meetings and had so many press conferences and interviews.

The next morning, as we rounded Diamond Head, we came upon the men who dive for money. I had never seen this done and it intrigued me so that I did not realize we were going into the harbor. Then I saw the Hawaiian band, all dressed in white, and heard the women singing "Aloha." I think it must be the most beautiful entrance anywhere in the world. When we had docked, many Hawaiians came on board with *leis*. We knew hardly anyone in Honolulu, and we did not expect any reception, but I think we ended up with somewhere around eighty *leis* among us. There was one *lei* made of the ginger flower and you never forget that odor.

In spite of this warm reception, I felt that I had to be very careful of what I said and did while I was there. I learned from some friends that there had been considerable opposition in some quarters to my coming because I was supposed to be a labor leader and the employers were afraid I would stir up trouble.

We got there about a week before the conference opened and had a fairly important part in formulating the program. Jane Addams was chairman of the conference and I was chairman of the industrial committee. We had many very interesting women as delegates. They came from Japan, China, Australia, New Zealand, Samoa, and Canada, and most of them were appointed by their governments.

In the meetings of the industrial committee I tried to get the delegates to report on the working conditions of the women in their countries. I felt it more important for us to learn the facts about actual conditions than just to talk about standards and generalities. We had a rather serious row when our committee wanted to report to the general conference our discussion of extraterritorial rights in China. An American woman, who had been in China and who thought she knew more about conditions there than anyone else, was very ag-

gressive in her determination that the matter of extraterritorial
rights should not be brought up in the general conference.
She came to me and said, "You can't talk about that." I replied, "I don't know why. It is one of the conditions that
affect employment in China." She said, "The Chinese government won't stand for it," but I answered, "I'll take the
responsibility myself, whether they stand for it or not."

I was on the executive committee and Jane Addams called
a meeting to discuss this matter. The American woman got
up and said that if we discussed extraterritorial rights, the
Chinese delegates would be beheaded when they got home.
Miss Addams was ready and she answered, "Why should they
be? They are part of the present government and that government is opposed to extraterritorial rights. I should think
the government would be very happy to have us discuss it."
Then Miss Addams said, "I will take it upon myself to defend
them if it is necessary, and I think I can. I know Dr. Sun Yat
Sen very well." Then we made our report to the general
conference and condemned extraterritorial rights.

Although the American woman insisted that the Chinese
delegates could not go back to China as a result of this report,
when the question came up of where the next meeting would
be held, she gave an invitation to the conference to meet in
China. This suggestion was met by a Chinese doctor, who took
the floor and made the speech of her life. She said it was time
for the Chinese women to speak for themselves, that they
were not ready to have any conferences, that when the right
time came the Chinese women themselves would issue the
invitation.

It was one of the best things that happened at the conference. The Chinese women asserted their right to speak for
themselves and we all applauded.

I think the meeting accomplished something. I think that
they all do. Those of us who were there got a different per-
spective on the situation in the Orient and on the women of
the Orient. The Chinese women were free, they could say

what they wanted and do what they wanted. The Japanese women were not free; they always had to be careful that they did not say anything that might be derogatory to the Japanese government. Their expenses were paid by the government, they were teachers under the government, and they were not free teachers. They were excellent women, but they themselves admitted they could not say anything that would at all reflect on the Japanese government.

This kind of thing is hard for us Americans to understand, but we must understand it if we are to know how to deal with people who live in countries where they do not have freedom.

We stayed more than a week after the conference and all the time I was there I had to do a good deal of speaking. I was urged by some people to talk about the problems of Hawaii. But, after having learned of the opposition to my coming there, I, of course, was particularly careful, and I always said that I did not know the conditions in Hawaii and so could not speak of them. Instead, I spoke of the conditions on the mainland and the importance of good standards for working conditions.

I think that when I left Honolulu I had won the employers' sympathy and they were never afraid of me afterward. I had a great deal of correspondence with many of them. It was an interesting and very happy experience.

The working conditions for women in Hawaii were bad in many ways. Not in the canneries, and not in the cane fields or the pineapple plants, but in the garment industry and in the restaurants, the hotels, and the service industries the conditions of employment were the most deplorable I have ever seen.

They did not have regular garment factories. Japanese workers made the garments in their own homes, with apprentices who worked, sometimes two years, for nothing, just to learn the trade. The restaurants paid nothing; the waitresses had to depend on tips. All these jobs resulted in great poverty. The saving grace of the whole situation was that there was perpetual summer. People did not have to have much clothing, nor did they have to wear shoes, but their poverty was awful just the same.

It seemed terrible to me that such conditions should exist in a country where there was so much beauty and where we were being entertained every day at the most wonderful parties, with delicious food, lovely music, and picturesque surroundings that were more beautiful than anything I had ever imagined.

When we got back to the United States we went to Los Angeles where I participated in one of the most picturesque ceremonies I had ever seen. I had to make a speech at Long Beach, where there was a big fair going on. Every day at the fair a special group was honored, and the day of my speech it was the Indians. When I arrived I was met by a delegation of women who gave me an enormous bouquet of dahlias. Then my honor escort of Indians appeared in full war paint and feathers. I had to march at the head of the parade, carrying my huge bouquet with the whole pack of Indians whooping at my back!

My next trip to foreign lands did not come until 1931. There was considerable excitement about that trip. I planned to go to Geneva at the time of the conference of the International Labor Organization. The United States was not a member of the International Labor Organization at that time and did not even send official observers, but I did not think there would be any harm in my being there to see what was going on. We had discovered that the National Woman's party was going to have representatives in Geneva for the conference to try to get endorsement of the equal rights principle, which would include opposition to all special legislation for women. Of course, we could not permit this to happen and we all felt it was important to have some active labor leader from the United States to present our side of the case. Fortunately, we were able to arrange that Elisabeth Christman should go, representing the National Women's Trade Union League.

The two of us started to make our plans. I talked over my idea with the secretary of labor, Mr. Doak. He thought I should go and the State Department gave me a passport. Just as I was about to sail, some enterprising reporter found out where I was going and asked the State Department if that meant that the United States was taking part in the International Labor Organization conference. Then the fat was in the fire.

I was already on board the ship when I received a telegram from the secretary's office telling me that I was not to go to Geneva or take any part in the conference. The people in my office were having a fit because they knew it was too late for me to change my plans for sailing and they did not know what I could do. When I got the telegram, I decided that so long as I did not appear officially in Geneva, it would be all right, and I went ahead with my itinerary as it had been originally planned. Of course, Elisabeth Christman could do what she wanted, not being a government official.

We took the night train from Paris to Geneva and wired my old friend Mary Dingman, international secretary of the YWCA, to meet me in Geneva the next morning. She and Evelyn Fox, one of her colleagues in the YWCA, smuggled me to their apartment, where I stayed overnight and met some of the women from the International Labor Organization secretariat. The next morning I was whisked up to the Hotel Bellevue on the Salève in France. Technically, I was not in Geneva. I was not even in Switzerland. But actually I was only a short distance by trolley from Geneva and all the time the conference was going on I stayed there and the women delegates to the conference came up to see me.

In the meantime, Elisabeth stayed in Geneva and did a splendid job with the labor delegates to the conference, explaining the issue involved in the Woman's party amendment so effectively that it was overwhelmingly defeated. So far as

I was concerned, my segregation on the Salève was an absurd situation, but it did not do any harm and I learned much and made a good many contacts that were very valuable to me when two years later, in 1933, I was appointed by President Roosevelt as chairman of the delegation of official United States observers at the International Labor Organization conference.

That time there was no secrecy about my presence in Geneva. Our delegation was welcomed very heartily, as an evidence that the United States was beginning to participate in the work of the international organization. The other members of our delegation were Dr. William Stead of the University of Minnesota, Edwin Smith of the department of labor in Massachusetts, and Hugh Franey from the American Federation of Labor. We did not have any representative of the employers because it was very difficult to get any important employers to leave the United States just then. They all wanted to be at home because the National Recovery Administration was just being set up and they were all very busy. The employers' representatives from other nations at the conference objected rather strenuously to their lack of representation in our delegation and I cabled the secretary of labor urging that our ambassador in France be asked to come. But he could not arrange to be there, and we ended up with no employers' delegate. It was really not very important because as advisers we had no vote in the conference. We could speak on any subject and attend any committee meetings, but our responsibility stopped there.

While the conference was going on, a dinner was given for our delegation, with Harold Butler, director of the International Labor Organization, presiding. At that dinner the story came out about my visit to the Salève in 1931. Finally, some of the English delegates said they would build a cottage there in honor of that episode because they thought that it was the beginning of American participation in the International Labor Organization.

I never imagined, when I talked to President Wilson in Paris about the need for getting the clause in the International Labor Organization constitution giving the right to women to participate in the work of the International Labor Organization, that I would be the first woman from the United States to have that opportunity, but that was how it worked out and it made me feel very proud. Since the United States joined the International Labor Organization in 1934 there has always been a woman as one of the government delegates.

23

Cooperation: Failures and Successes

DURING all the time I was director of the Women's Bureau, I was constantly working with the various women's organizations that were interested in general social problems. I imagine that about half my time was spent at meetings, making speeches, trying to arouse interest in the problems of women in industry, and serving on committees for one thing or another. I found it rather difficult at first, because until I came to Washington I had almost always worked directly with labor groups or with people who were especially concerned with industrial problems. But as director of the Women's Bureau I found that almost all women's organizations were interested in our program and they were often very helpful in pushing for what we thought should be done. Even when their program did not include any direct action on women in industry, I was often asked to take part in their meetings and I did so because I felt I had a responsibility to carry out that should not be limited to any special groups.

One of the first general women's organizations that I became interested in was the Conference on the Cause and Cure of War. This organization started soon after the close of World War I and was intended to be a kind of educational movement with membership open to any organization inter-

ested in promoting study of the causes and prevention of
war. Mrs. Carrie Chapman Catt was the chairman and the
organization met annually in Washington. I was in Buffalo at
the original luncheon meeting when the organization was
formed and I took part in its meetings and helped plan its
program for the years it was in existence.

The first "Cause and Cure" meetings did not get a very
friendly response from the public. The newspapers made
fun of them and they were attacked by so-called patriotic
organizations and other conservative groups. But Mrs. Catt
and the fine people who worked with her were not disturbed
by this and kept on planning study programs and stimulating
women's groups to educate themselves on political and international affairs. Each year the attendance grew larger and
the speakers more distinguished, until finally the members
of the Cabinet and the State Department gave it their endorsement and the meetings had real importance. The organization
continued until shortly before World War II. I think it did
some very effective work though I always felt it never took
all the causes of war into consideration. It kept pretty much
to the political field and did not go into economic problems,
which I think are probably the biggest causes of war. However, many women's organizations that had never thought of
international or political problems before began to study and
read about them, so something was accomplished.

One of the most interesting of the women's organizations
and one that worked closely with us for all the years I was in
the bureau is the Women's Joint Congressional Committee.
This committee was organized soon after the woman's suf-
rage amendment was passed and its first chairman was Mrs.
Maud Wood Park, the famous suffrage leader and organizer
of the League of Women Voters. The Women's Joint Congressional Committee is a clearinghouse of national women's
organizations that are interested in supporting or defeating
bills presented in the federal Congress. The member organizations of the committee that are working for the same bill pool

their information and plan their strategy together so there is less duplication and more effective pressure brought to bear on the members of Congress.

There was always a committee of the "Women's Joint," as we called it, that was interested in getting larger appropriations for the Women's Bureau. Year after year they appeared before the Bureau of the Budget or the Appropriations committees in Congress and supported our request for additional funds. They worked hard for us and I was always very grateful to them.

It is hard to tell how effective their efforts were. I think that any pressure from outside is always helpful, but usually that is not enough. To really get something from an appropriation committee you have to have some member of the committee itself who is interested and will go to bat for you. But I am sure the general interest and endorsement of our work by the women's organizations were helpful in the long run. We began the Women's Bureau with an appropriation of $30,000 a year. Gradually our funds were increased until we were getting $150,000. We stayed at about that amount until the last few years I was with the bureau. Just before I retired we got an increase that brought our total to more than $246,000. This was not enough for all the things we wanted to do that should be done, but anyway it represented a steady increase which was encouraging.

With the exception of Mrs. Edith Nourse Rogers, representative from Massachusetts, the women in Congress were never especially helpful to the bureau in getting appropriations. Mrs. Rogers was really interested and gave us much useful advice and support, but, as a group, the women representatives were apt to be already interested in some special subject when they came to Congress and it took a while for them to find out about us.

In the early days of the Women's Bureau, I became a member of the National Conference of Social Work and I have been a member ever since. I belonged to the Industrial Section, as it was called at that time. At first, the social workers were not much interested in industrial problems. When the Industrial Section met there would be only a few people, although the conference had many thousands of members. That kept on for some years, but in 1929 and 1930 when the depression started, our section was unusually well attended. The social workers had begun to realize that the problems of social work had something in common with the economic situation and they were very anxious to know what was going to be done and what could be done. They knew that relief was not the answer and that something more fundamental had to be done.

Then the conference reorganized into five sections. Section four became the Social and Economic Section and I was made vice-chairman of it. A short time later the chairman died and I became the chairman, which meant that I had to meet with the chairmen of the other sections and formulate the program for the next conference.

My cue, of course, was to work up a liberal program. The conference was to be held in Kansas City. I thought I had a very good program. Mary van Kleeck was one of our speakers. She was considered at that time to be the leader of the younger and more radical element among the social workers and was very popular at the conference. In an earlier speech she had advocated action to deal with the depression that Harry Hopkins later took strong exception to. The delegates to the conference had looked forward to Mr. Hopkins' speech because as director of the WPA they expected a good deal from him. Instead of that, he used the occasion to say nothing in general and very much against Miss van Kleeck in particular.

The conference was very angry. Miss van Kleeck was to make her speech at my section the next morning and everyone turned out to hear her. When I went to the hall assigned to us the crowd was so big that we had to move over to the big Conference Hall. It was packed. I think almost all the members of the conference were there. Miss van Kleeck made an excellent speech and was acclaimed by the whole conference. She ignored the statements that Hopkins had made the night before and talked instead about the philosophy of the industrial situation.

At the Kansas City conference I was elected chairman of section four. The next conference was in Indianapolis. It was not as big a conference as usual because people were not drawn toward that city and the hotel accommodations were very poor. We had more or less the usual routine and as far as section four was concerned, our program hinged on economics and industrial conditions. Miss van Kleeck was on the program again and made a very good speech, as usual. We had large meetings all the time — overflowing.

For the Saturday morning meeting I had asked Miss Perkins, the secretary of labor, to speak. She had promised she would come, but on Friday afternoon about four o'clock I got a telegram saying that she could not come but was sending her speech, which was to be about the International Labor Organization. I said to Miss van Kleeck, "I don't know whether that speech will get here for the meeting tomorrow morning or not. If it doesn't, you have got to make the speech for me." She agreed to help me out.

Saturday morning came and I did not receive the speech from Secretary Perkins. In the meantime, we had to give out to the papers that the secretary was not coming and that Miss van Kleeck was going to take her place. I don't think that the secretary of the conference was very pleased, but there was nothing else we could do.

Again we had an audience of about two thousand people and Miss van Kleeck gave a fine speech on the International Labor Organization about which she had a great deal of information and many constructive ideas.

It was quite a trick to get up these programs. The chairmen of the sections met every month, so that we could coordinate the sectional programs as a whole to avoid repetition and get a well-rounded discussion. I always felt that Howard R. Knight, the secretary, did an excellent job of coordination. We also had to get speakers who would pay their own expenses, or whose organizations paid them. Therefore, although we usually had a fairly wide range of good speakers, they often dropped out and we had to find substitutes.

I continued on the Social and Economic Section of the conference for a number of years and the attendance at our meetings grew until it became one of the most important sections. We always tried to have the kind of program on industrial questions that would be enlightening to the social worker and I believe that we were successful. I think that social workers have always had a tendency to get buried under their work, not realizing that most social work is really only a stopgap and what we should do is attack the more fundamental social problems and diminish the need for social workers. I hope the programs of my section did something to further this point of view.

On the whole, I have a great deal of respect for social work. I know that we must have it, but I know too that the social worker has become so professional that there is overemphasis on the profession, rather than on the work itself. I know that there had to be much higher standards and a more professional attitude among the workers and for the work than there was in the beginning, but it seems to me that, at least in some places, there is an overemphasis on technique. I am not against social work's becoming a profession; I think that is what it should be. But I think there is always a danger of overprofessionalizing.

One completely unsuccessful movement that I took part in was the attempt to set up a woman's charter that would be accepted by all women's organizations. In 1936 when the agitation for the equal rights amendment was very intense, several of us felt that we should have a conference with the women's organizations that were opposed to the amendment and see if we could not set up a positive program to work for, instead of just opposing the amendment.

This conference was held in New York at the Russell Sage Foundation. Mary van Kleeck was really the instigator of this meeting and she was present as an adviser. Others present were representatives of the Young Women's Christian Association, the General Federation of Women's Clubs, the League of Women Voters, the National Council of Catholic Women, the Business and Professional Women's clubs, and the National Women's Trade Union League. We decided at that meeting to draw up a positive program that we could all work for and to call it the Woman's Charter. It took a good many meetings and much discussion before we got a wording for the charter that we could all agree to. When it was in final form we were very pleased with it and we hoped that at last we had something that all women could endorse and work for and that perhaps we could, with this charter, bridge the gap between ourselves and the National Woman's party. It was an excellent statement. There was almost nothing in it that anyone could take exception to and we hoped it might prove to be a rallying point for women all over the world. It said:

This Charter is a general statement of the social and economic objectives of women, for women and for society as a whole, insofar as these can be embodied in legislation and governmental administration. It is put forward in order that there may be an agreed formulation of the purposes to which a large number of women's organizations throughout the world already are committed. It is recognized that some of the present specific needs which it seeks to remedy should disappear as society develops the assurance of a more complete life for every person; and some of its objectives would establish conditions which should be attainable for all persons, so that in promoting them for women it is hoped thereby to bring nearer the time of their establishment for all.

Women shall have full political and civil rights; full opportunity for education; full opportunity for work according to their individual abilities, with safeguards against physically harmful conditions of employment and economic exploitation; they shall receive compensation, without discrimination because of sex. They shall be assured security of livelihood, including the safeguarding of motherhood. The provisions necessary for the establishment of these standards, shall be guaranteed by government, which shall insure also the right of united action toward the attainment of these aims.

Where special exploitation of women workers exists, such as low wages which provide less than the living standards attainable, unhealthful working conditions, or long hours of work which result in physical exhaustion and denial of the right to leisure, such conditions shall be corrected through social and labor legislation, which the world's experience shows to be necessary.

Some of us contributed a little money and we had thousands of copies of the charter printed and set about to get it discussed and adopted by all kinds of women's organizations.

But nothing worked out the way we had wanted it to. The movement was a complete flop. The Woman's party would not have anything to do with it. In fact, they attacked it because of the clause about special legislation for women. The various women's organizations could not endorse it without long periods of study and action by their membership. The makeup of their organizations was such that they could not submerge themselves in a joint program with a number of other organizations. Generally this is a good idea. I think it is important for an organization to be directed by its membership and not just by its board of directors. The membership should know just what the program is and should be back of each item on it. This cannot be done in important organizations with thousands of members without spending much time to inform individual members and get them to express their wishes. I think it is a good plan to adopt a national program and hold fast to it. But there are always emergencies coming up that have to be taken care of and it is a mistake to have a program so tight that it cannot ever be deviated from.

This was the chief snag that the Woman's Charter struck. It cut across too many programs of the national women's organizations. No one group would take responsibility for it and the national organizations could not act jointly because of the limitations of their setups. The National Women's Trade Union League took much of the responsibility for distributing the charter and we all held meetings and had endless discussions about it, but in the end it came to nothing.

At the time of the Textile Conference held under the auspices of the International Labor Organization in Washington in April 1937, we felt that the ILO should pass a resolution that embodied some of the principles of the charter. We wanted it especially to go on record for special legislation for women. Since there were a number of ILO officials at the Textile Conference, we thought it was an opportune moment to discuss the wording of a resolution with them. We were fortunate in getting the assistance of Edward Phelan, the assistant director of the ILO, who helped us with the wording of the resolution.

Grace Abbott, chief of the Children's Bureau, was one of the United States government delegates at the next meeting of the ILO in June 1937. We got the secretary of labor to instruct Miss Abbott to present this resolution, although she did not want to do it. It was finally adopted almost as it was presented.

Whereas, in view of the social and political changes of recent years and the fact that women workers have suffered from special forms of exploitation and discrimination in the past, there is need to re-examine their general position; and

Whereas, it is for the best interests of society that in addition to full political and civil rights and full opportunity for education, women should have full opportunity to work and should receive remuneration without discrimination because of sex, and be protected by legislative safeguards against physically harmful conditions of employment and economic exploitation, including the safeguarding of motherhood; and

Whereas, it is necessary that women as well as men should be guaranteed freedom of association by Governments and should be protected by social and labour legislation which world experience has shown to be effective in abolishing special exploitation of women workers; therefore be it

Resolved, that the Twenty-third Session of the International Labour Conference, while recognizing that some of these principles lie within the competence of other International bodies, believes them to be of the greatest importance to workers in general and especially to women workers; and therefore requests the Governing Body to draw them to the attention of all Governments, with a view to their establishment in law and in custom by legislative and administrative action.

I think this is the most effective way to get this type of resolution passed. On the basis of the Woman's Charter one or two of us individually formulated the resolution, got advice from qualified people about it, and then persuaded the various organizations to back it. If we had waited for all the organizations to get together and formulate something they would all stand back of, we would have gotten nowhere, as the Woman's Charter campaign showed.

Later on, at the time of the San Francisco meeting to form the United Nations, we did the same thing again. A couple of us decided that there should be a specific statement in the charter of the United Nations that would guarantee the eligibility of women for all positions in the organization. We drafted the statement we felt should go in, took it to Edward Stettinius, the secretary of state, and to Dean Virginia Gildersleeve; the women's organizations endorsed it when there was discussion of it in San Francisco and it was incorporated in the United Nations Charter in almost the words we had suggested: "The United Nations shall place no restrictions on the eligibility of men and women to participate in any capacity and under conditions of equality in its principal and subsidiary organs."

New Quarters and New Friends

IN June 1930 we celebrated the tenth anniversary of the Women's Bureau. We did not have a formal celebration, just a supper party for all the members of the staff. It was a very jolly gathering. We were all friends together and we were proud of what we had accomplished in ten years. Mary van Kleeck could not be with us, but she sent a lovely letter, a part of which I will quote here, not because of the nice things she said about me, but because she said so much better than I can what the bureau as a whole stood for.

I wish that I could be with you at the party — for I would so love to try to express to Mary Anderson something of my feeling about her leadership. She knows that I love her personally. I don't believe she knows how great is my pride in her work — "my" pride being only my expression of a feeling that every woman in the United States must have in Mary Anderson's wise judgment, steadiness of purpose and deep spirit of kinship with all women in industry — born out of her own industrial experience. And in paying tribute to her leadership we enhance it, as she would agree, when we say that she could not have done it alone. For the Women's Bureau is bigger than any one person; it is that priceless thing — a co-operative product. Into its achievements have gone the loyalty of Ann Larrabee, (You see how important I consider a secretary, and it is in that capacity that I knew her first;), the breezy Western experience which Agnes

Peterson and Caroline Manning brought to an otherwise effete East; Ethel Best's tireless curiosity and ingenuity in devising new questions; Mary Winslow's skill in planning — and if I leave much unsaid about each of them, and omit many who should be named with them, it is only because they are symbols of the fine spirit for the devotion and intelligence which is the Women's Bureau.

My love to her collectively and individually, and may the next ten years be richly blessed.

Shortly after our tenth anniversary we had a real catastrophe in the bureau that showed up the fine quality of our staff. On a hot day in September 1931 the building in which we had our offices burned to the ground. It was a very ramshackle old building, one of the temporary ones that had been built for the wartime emergency and there was no fire protection at all. Fortunately, it happened on a Saturday afternoon so no one was hurt, but many of our, precious records went up in flames. We were working at the time on a very large investigation for which we had thousands of schedules all ready for the statistical machines. Since these cards were tightly packed in boxes, they were not very inflammable. The girls decided that they could be salvaged from the ruins of the building; as soon as they were allowed to they started digging away the ashes and eventually found almost all the schedules. They cleaned the ashes and smoke stains off them and we were able to complete our report. If it had not been for the devotion and hard work of these girls, all the time and effort spent in collecting the information on the schedules would have gone to nothing.

After the fire we moved into another temporary building, where we were very uncomfortable. The building was in wretched condition. During the year and a half we were in it the foundation had to be renewed twice. The new building for the Public Health Service was being constructed just across the street. The noise of riveting was so loud we could not get much work done and we were delighted when finally our building cracked so badly we had to move out.

We next went to the Little building on F Street, near Seventeenth. This was a well-constructed building and no one was in it but ourselves. It was a haven after all we had been through and it had the advantage of being right back of the Department of Labor, so that when I was called over for conferences, I did not have far to go. We stayed there until December 1933 when we made our last move into the new Department of Labor building on Constitution Avenue and Fourteenth Street.

In that building we had quite a time getting the kind of offices we wanted allocated to us by the chief clerk of the department. At first, he wanted to give me an office in the darkest corner of the building where all the work would have to be done by electric light. He said it was a specially good room because it had a full bathroom attached to it! I objected very much to being put there and finally compromised on another office with no bathroom, just a wash basin in the corner, but with plenty of light and air.

The new building was very comfortable — air cooled and some of it soundproof. It was fine for the workers of the country to have such a dignified and important building for their department. I felt proud when we finally were settled in our new quarters. My office was a big and beautiful room. The high ceiling was soundproof and the windows were enormous, so I had plenty of light. All the furniture was mahogany with green leather upholstery and a soft green carpet to match. My secretary was in an outer office. I was alone and I was almost lost in that big room, but I always kept my doors open so that no one would feel shut out. I think the peace and quiet of that office was a great help to me in the turbulent years that followed.

By the time we moved into the new building the Roosevelt administration was in full swing and I began to see quite a bit of Mrs. Roosevelt. Of course, I had known her for many years, but now that she was in the White House and was so much interested in all the problems we were dealing with, our meetings were much more frequent. Her friendliness and interest in our work were a very great help. One of the first things she did when she became the First Lady of the land was to have a series of receptions for the women in government service, who had never before been particularly recognized by the White House or by other government officials. Invitations were usually limited to the men officials and their wives and a very few of the top women officials. But Mrs. Roosevelt changed that and started to have garden parties in the spring for the women. They were very beautiful parties, with the Marine Band playing on the green lawn and thousands of women in their summer clothes. It was a fine gesture and the women appreciated it.

One day I got word from Mrs. Roosevelt asking me to receive with her to represent the Department of Labor, because Miss Perkins was out of town. Of course, I was very glad to do this, but I found it was an ordeal. I think we had nearly two thousand people at that party and everyone had to shake our hands. In the receiving line were Mrs. Roosevelt and the Cabinet ladies and myself. I finally got so that I could not even see the guests as we greeted them. They went by as a blank. My hand was swollen for days afterward. I do not see how Mrs. Roosevelt managed to keep on doing that kind of thing for so many years. I think she had a special faculty for meeting people. No matter how many hands she had shaken, she always made you feel when your turn came that she knew you and was glad to see you.

Another thing Mrs. Roosevelt did that I think was very important was holding her weekly press conferences. These were an innovation too. One of the members of our staff always attended these conferences and from time to time Mrs. Roosevelt would invite me or another woman to discuss some topic that was of interest. This was very helpful as it gave us an opportunity to explain things to the women reporters and in this way they often got stories that the men did not get.

I will never forget one party that Mrs. Roosevelt gave for the women of the press. I had just come back from New York and was told that she had been trying to reach me. I called the White House and she said, "Mary, I want you to take part in the stunt party that we are going to give for the press women. Miss Perkins cannot be present and I want you to take her part and represent labor. I am going to send you the program and the lines that you are to speak. We will have two rehearsals. You must come as a laborer, or a working man."

I did not know exactly what to do, but I called a friend who was a railroad man to find out how to dress. He told me what to get and where to get it. I did not know at that time that there was a well-defined railroad garb. I had to have a pair of overalls with a six-inch cuff on the bottom to keep the cinders from blowing up; a blue shirt and a handkerchief tied around my neck to keep the cinders from going down; also a special cap with a big visor, to shield my eyes from glaring light and cinders; a regular overall jacket, and a pair of gloves with long cuffs, so the cinders would not go up the sleeves.

For the second rehearsal we had to wear our costumes. We took them to a room in the White House and changed there. I thought that I would be the only one with overalls on, but I found that Mrs. Wallace was in overalls to represent a farmer. Mrs. Swanson, wife of the secretary of the navy, had on a sailor suit. The wife of the assistant postmaster general had on a letter carrier's suit and Mrs. Woodring, the wife of the secretary of war, wore a West Point cadet uniform. When I saw them I didn't feel so alone in men's clothes. All I had to do was walk on the stage and salute and then stand back. The President came in to watch us at the second rehearsal. He laughed heartily and also told us what we did wrong. The party itself was a great success. All enjoyed themselves and I think it established a very cordial feeling among us all.

Probably the most interesting party I ever went to at the White House was later on, in 1939, when the king and queen of England were staying there. One day before they arrived I got a note from Mrs. Roosevelt saying that, if it met with the approval of the king and queen, they were inviting to the White House a few people from the government whom they thought the king and queen would be interested to meet. Mrs. Roosevelt asked if I would be willing to come and talk about my work. Of course, I sent back word that I would come. I was told not to mention the fact that I was going because the press was not being invited.

When the time came, Katharine Lenroot, chief of the Children's Bureau, and I went to the White House together. As we went in all the newspaper people were standing in a crowd outside the gate to see who had been invited. We assembled in the White House and then moved out onto the lawn where tea was served. I walked out with Admiral Richard E. Byrd. We were introduced to the king and queen and, in American fashion, we shook hands. I was glad that I did not have to curtsy.

After that I wandered around a bit. I did not see the President, who was in a chair on the lawn a little apart from the others. All of a sudden I heard a plaintive voice saying, "Aren't you going to speak to me?" I answered that I certainly was going to speak and he took both my hands and said, "I knew you would."

I did not talk to the king, but Mrs. Roosevelt called me and introduced me to the queen, saying, "She knows Margaret Bondfield very well." This was my cue, so I talked about Margaret for a minute or two. The queen said she remembered that when Margaret had come back from the United States she had told her a good deal about soil erosion. I knew that it must have been the Tennessee Valley Authority that Margaret had talked about, because she had been so much interested in it while she was here, and I told the queen something about it. As soon as I could I switched to my own work.

She seemed interested and said, "I understand you are having trouble about married women working. I am in favor of women doing what they want to do." This remark gave me a lot of confidence in her. I felt that she was not only lovely and gracious, but that she would be a stanch friend of women. I think, so far as she has been able to, that is what she has been through all the terrible years of the war and the difficult years since.

25

The Bryn Mawr Summer School

LONG before I was director of the Women's Bureau, Mrs. Robins, with her usual forethought for working women and her dynamic way of planning, had proposed a resolution to the National Women's Trade Union League, at their conference in 1916, that the women's colleges should open up summer schools for the education of women in industry. This resolution was adopted and the agitation for this kind of workers' education began. But it was not until some years later that anything came of it.

Eventually, however, one day in 1921, I had word that Dr. M. Carey Thomas, who was the president of Bryn Mawr College, and Dr. Susan Kingsbury, who was a professor there, wanted to see me. We met in my office and Dr. Thomas told me that they wanted to start a summer school for women in industry to be held at Bryn Mawr College. She said that she had been inspired with this idea the summer before when she was living in a villa looking down over Constantinople. Since Mrs. Robins and the Women's Trade Union League had been working for such a plan for many years, I knew it would have their support and I was enthusiastic about Dr. Thomas' suggestion. She told me that she had already discussed it with Dr. Felix Frankfurter of Harvard and that he had suggested she come to see me. We talked over possibilities and not long afterward we had an organizational meeting in Dr. Thomas' home, the Deanery in Bryn Mawr.

At that meeting there were representatives of nearly all the women's organizations, including working women and the alumnae of Bryn Mawr. Elisabeth Christman represented the Women's Trade Union League. It was a most impressive and interesting group. Our purpose was to set up a general committee to work out the program and also to set up special committees to handle admissions and other specific functions. I was asked to be on the admissions committee.

Our plan was that the girls should come to Bryn Mawr for two months in the summer and that all their expenses would be paid; we knew that none of the girls could come unless we provided for them. Even so, it would be something of a sacrifice for them, because they would lose their pay during those months and there was also the question of whether their employers would let them come back if they left their jobs.

We started out by having seventy-five girls. We wanted one hundred, but were able to recruit only seventy-five from all parts of the country. Some of the girls could not leave home because they were the sole support of their families and could not afford to lose their wages; others had other responsibilities. Some girls were afraid to come. We also had to see that they had an eighth-grade education, though we would take exceptional girls with less. We lowered that standard later on, because so many of the women in the South had gone to work before they had finished the eighth grade.

We recruited mostly through the Young Women's Christian Association and the trade unions. In the South the YWCA was probably the best source of information because many of the girls were members of the Industrial Division of the YWCA and its workers knew them better than we did. Wherever the Women's Trade Union League had a local, it would recommend some women. In Chicago, New York, and Boston, we took almost entirely the Trade Union League Women. We also had to get the cooperation of the employers.

We set up committees to select candidates in the different sections of the country. I was chairman of the southern committee for a number of years, so my experience was mostly with the southern girls. There we had no Women's Trade Union League to help us. We found we had to change the method of recruiting for each area.

At first, in selecting the girls, we planned to take one from an industry each year, but then we realized that when the girls went back to their work they were rather lonely and set aside from the others because they had "gone to college." In the South, a girl who had been to the summer school was always watched a good deal by her employer because he would be afraid she had learned things from the trade union girls from Chicago, New York, and Boston.

Our idea was that the girl trained at the summer school should become a leader in her community, but in the South she rarely got a chance for leadership. The workers in the southern factories were not ready to organize in any way and indeed could not do so because they were held down by the employers. Therefore the girl who knew more than the other workers did was often avoided. The other girls were afraid to associate with her because they might lose their jobs.

Because of this we changed our method of recruiting and tried to get at least five girls from one city so as to have a nucleus in different areas. There were a great many differences of opinion about this on the admissions committee, but I held out for the nucleus. And it worked better.

After we had selected the first students and the summer school started, there was a great deal of unrest among the students because there were some girls who had no preparation whatsoever for any group action, while the trade union girls from Baltimore and New York were united in a feeling that workers were not adequately represented on the committee that was running the school. They wanted to have fifty per cent representation on this committee; this was opposed very strongly by Dr. Thomas. We were not able to adjust representation that year and this caused a great deal of dissatisfaction among the students, some of whom objected to the academic courses and to a few of the teachers.

When this agitation was at its height, I was called in Washington one day and asked if I would come to Bryn Mawr to tell the girls what we were trying to do and explain that the school was not set up to agitate for trade unionism, but to provide training to help them do their work, whatever it was, in their communities.

I went, and I think I spoke very plainly that day. I know that some of the teachers told me that they would not have dared to say what I said to the girls. I saw that the girls were mistaken in their ideas and I talked to them as to another worker. I said that this was not the place for trade union agitation, but a place to learn what they could through the different courses. The girls finally accepted my explanations and then it came out all right, but we certainly had an hour's plain talk. They came back at me in good old trade union fashion, but I had been accustomed to that for years, and I knew how to take it.

Then the next year the same question came up again, whether there should be 50–50 representation on the committee. The board of directors argued one whole morning and I remember resenting very much statements of Mrs. Bertrand Russell, who was a cousin of Dr. Thomas. She argued with us about the 50–50 plan, saying, "What would the working woman know about academic education?" I said it was not academic education we were trying to give the girls, but rather information that would be useful in their everyday lives. We felt they knew what they needed and that they had certainly shown this in their studies at the school.

When we adjourned for lunch that day, Dr. Thomas came to me and said, "Won't you sit with me for lunch and pick out some of the girls to join us? I want them to sit with me because I want to discuss this with them." I selected several girls and we all sat together. One of the girls from Baltimore talked all the time with Dr. Thomas, explaining the workers' side. After the luncheon I asked the girls to come together and suggested, "Don't you think, since Dr. Thomas has been so fine about everything, we might drop this controversy until some time later?" They agreed and asked me to announce this before the meeting began again. But I did not have a chance to make the announcement, or even to get the floor, before Dr. Thomas got up and said, "I have decided that there should be 50–50 representation." And what she decided went.

Another difficulty we had during the first days of the summer school was with the working hours for the employees of the college. Dr. Thomas thought they should keep the usual staff of chambermaids and waitresses, because the girls at the summer school should have a holiday from housework and should live as nearly as possible the way the regular college girls lived. I warned Dr. Thomas that if they kept these employees they had better look after their working conditions and give them an eight-hour day and sufficient wages, or there would be trouble.

It was a little difficult for Bryn Mawr to put the eight-hour day into effect, because they did not have that for the winter employees. Dr. Thomas and her staff argued that if they established it in the summer they would have to do it in the winter too. We said, "Why not?" We did not think it would be too difficult to work out a schedule, but they did not get around to doing it and I thought some of the trade union girls who came to the school would agitate for it. Dr. Thomas said, "We'll have to see what happens."

Sure enough, after the girls were there for a few days, they found out that the workers had a long day and they set to work to organize them. Then the household workers spoke for themselves and the students aided them. It almost came to a strike, but finally we worked out a schedule for an eight-hour day for the summer and winter employees too. After that everything was serene.

The students were taught by professors and tutors recruited from Bryn Mawr and other colleges. Their courses included

English, economics, history, and labor legislation. They also had many discussion groups and lectures and some time was spent on recreation, because they had had little chance to learn to play.

One of the biggest problems we had to deal with at the school was the admission of Negro women students. During the third or fourth year we admitted three Negro women from Chicago, one from a lampshade factory and two household workers. This was all right with everyone but the girls from the South, who were a little difficult at first. We had to deal very carefully with them. When they arrived at the station in Bryn Mawr, one of the staff met them and told them that there were three very fine colored women coming to the school whom they would meet as soon as they got to the college.

One of the girls said, "Well, if that is so, I don't dare stay here. There would be too much fuss at home if they heard I was going to school with Negroes. I'll have to go right back." But she was persuaded to go on to the college and when she was settled in her room she met the other students, the colored girls with them, and decided that she would not go home after all. On the whole, there was no reaction against our having colored students and although Dr. Thomas was against it in the beginning, when she was once convinced, she gave in very gracefully.

I really enjoyed my contacts with Dr. Thomas. She was very sure of herself and very enthusiastic about every new idea she took up; at the same time she was the most graceful hostess I have ever met. I will never forget one meeting of the summer school committee held at the Deanery. Dr. Thomas had just "discovered" D. H. Lawrence, and she felt that everyone should read his books. She told us we must read *Sons and Lovers.* I had already read it because a short time before, when I was on vacation with Mary van Kleeck on a ranch near Taos in New Mexico, we had seen quite a bit of Lawrence and his wife, Frieda. They used to come over every

day to our ranch to get milk and cream and one day they
invited us to have tea with them. We got our ponies and rode
over to their ranch, where we found them all covered with
paint because they had just taken up "finger painting."
Neither Mary nor I had read any of Lawrence's books then,
but we were told he never wanted to discuss his books, so
we did not worry about that. Both he and Frieda were most
charming hosts. I was very interested in them both and later
on I read some of his books and Frieda's book too. I saw
Frieda again a few years ago when I was visiting in Albu-
querque. She remembered me and said, "If you ever have time
for a vacation, come out and stay with me." She was just the
same as before, the kind of warm person that you take to
immediately.

I did not tell Dr. Thomas that I already knew Lawrence.
She was so enthusiastic about her discovery I thought it was
kinder to let it go. Anyway, I know him more as a person
than as a writer.

The summer school was continued at Bryn Mawr for ten
years. Then it was moved to New York State where it still
continues in the summer months as the Hudson Shore Workers School. More recent developments have given an opportunity for longer periods of instruction and classes than were
possible in the two months of the summer vacation at Bryn
Mawr. Since the years it was carried on at Bryn Mawr there
has been an important progress in workers' education through
the unions and through summer schools for workers in other
colleges and I think on the whole the experiment at Bryn
Mawr had a good deal to do with this. Almost every girl who
went to the school became, if not a leader, at least a worker
in some civic organization. Many of them became real leaders
in the trade union movement. The director of the school was
Hilda Smith, who had before that been dean of the college.
The success of the school was chiefly due to her ability and
to Dr. Thomas' faith in her.

I think I was especially interested in the Bryn Mawr summer school because I, myself, had been so much helped by the educational program of the National Women's Trade Union League in the early days in Chicago. The summer school was effective, it got results, but on the whole, for the present time, I do not think such schools are the answer to workers' education. I think that this kind of education should be run by the workers themselves. There are things that are necessary to the workers that they cannot learn in any regular school system. I think our philosophy should be that education for trade unionists is a union responsibility. Any union that is worth its salt wants its members to understand the philosophy of the trade union movement, and I do not think this can be taught very well except under the auspices of the trade unions. A certain amount of academic education for all citizens is the responsibility of the state, but special education in the meaning and techniques of trade unionism can only come from the unions themselves.

26

Home Life in Washington

WHILE all these things were going on I got really established in Washington and began to have a very pleasant home life. As soon as I knew that I was going to be more or less permanently in Washington, I gave up my apartment in Chicago and brought my sister Anna to live with me. She was not very well and I thought she would be better off if she came to Washington. She kept house for the two of us and we had a very happy time together. We lived in apartments in various parts of the city, ending up in a very comfortable one at the Broadmoor on Connecticut Avenue. I had bought a car, a Ford sedan, very early in the game in 1919 and when I got through work in the afternoon I used to take my sister for lovely drives through the Washington parks.

Mary, my sister's daughter, was very fond of dogs. She had a male and a female Eskimo spitz. While I was in Chicago one time the female had pups and Mary said she was going to send one to her mother. When I got back to Washington I asked my sister if she really wanted the puppy. "Can you care for it? Because I know I can't help with it." My sister replied, "If she wants to send it, let her send it."

On my next trip I came back with a six-week-old puppy. I never saw anything as lovable in my life. He just waddled over the floor. He grew up to be quite a dog. When he was full grown, he had a yellow sheen in his white fur which made him very handsome. We kept him clean and washed up, because he had to stay in the apartment with us. He had a habit of walking on his hind legs. The first time I saw him do it was when we were expecting company and the table was all set. He walked on his hind legs all around the table to see what was there. He put me in mind of a little bear.

He was used to an apartment and to the elevator and the car. He would get off the elevator and walk on his hind legs all the way through the reception room on the first floor to the front door. Many times we were offered money for him. Once a man offered me three hundred dollars, but we said he was not for sale. He was the only dog we ever had except for a dog we had had when I was home in Sweden.

We called him Bobby. He was very devoted to my sister and when she was ill and lying on the sofa, he would get between the doctor and her to protect her. When I came home in the evening to take my sister for a ride, it was a jollification for Bobby. He would jump on the beds and the sofa and chairs and would sit at the door for an hour before I came. Then I would say to my sister, "I'll take Bobby out the back way while you go out the front." We would start down the back stairway but Bobby would run back and forth and would not go down with me until she opened the door and came out. He was the nicest pet I ever had and I was very unhappy when he was killed by an automobile after we had had him for eight years.

Before we left Chicago we had another pet that I was very fond of. He was a yellow canary named Pete. We used to let him out of the cage to fly around the apartment and we loved his singing. One evening, after we had had him for a few years, we went to a movie, and when we came back Pete was gone. We had forgotten to put him back in the cage and had left the dining room window open. We called and called and walked around half the night, knowing he had never been outdoors and would not be able to take care of himself. The next morning I said, "Before we leave, let's put some bread crumbs on the sill and leave the window open. Maybe he'll come back." I was in the bedroom and my sister was getting breakfast, when all of a sudden, Pete came in and flew around and around me and then went right over to my sister. I rushed and closed the window. He and we were so happy.

When we moved to Washington we did not want to take him with us. He was very old and had quit singing entirely. We gave him to some friends who had two little girls. They took such good care of him that he began to sing again. When he died, they had him stuffed and kept him.

When I was a young girl, I became fond of pigs. I like the way they eat and root. They can be pretty mean too, if they get mad, particularly if the sow has little ones. I think they are very interesting animals. In fact I like all animals, but Bobby and Pete were the only pets I ever had.

With my sister to keep house for me, with my car and Bobby and all the good friends I made in Washington, life was very pleasant but, of course, like everyone else, I always wanted a bit more than I had. So during the late twenties when the Florida boom was on I tried to make some money.

Elisabeth Christman had been in Florida visiting Mrs. Raymond Robins and she came back with lurid tales about how much people could make if they invested in Florida real estate. Mrs. Robins warned us against it, but several of us got very enthusiastic and decided to go into it together. A friend of ours in Chicago was in the real estate business and had made a good deal of money in Florida; we gave her our money and she invested it in some lots in Miami Beach and in a place called Palm Dale. I got about five of the Palm Dale lots, but they did not turn out to be worth anything. Later on, after paying small taxes every year, I asked a friend who was going to Florida to try to find out about these lots. He found that they were worthless, nothing but grazing land, so I stopped paying taxes and that was the end of my real estate venture.

My next money-making scheme was just as disastrous. A

friend of mine was selling shares in silver foxes that were being raised on a farm. I bought a pair, a male and a female, for sixteen hundred dollars. The idea was that when they started having pups I would sell the offspring for lots of money. After some time, they had four pups, but in the meantime, we were in the depression and there was no sale for furs. I had four pups which I could not get rid of. Eventually, I sold a couple of them for almost nothing. Then my friend was killed in an automobile accident and the farm manager stole the pups that were left and there was no way to prosecute him. Finally, the man who took over the farm wrote to me and said my pair had become sterile and asked if he should kill them and send me the furs. I agreed and he sent me two beautiful skins, but I had to pay for curing and mounting them. I sold one of them for fifty dollars and kept the other for myself, but I could not bear to wear it because I did not want to be reminded of that foolish transaction.

I made my last financial experiment when the railroad trainmen started a bank in Cleveland. Many people became interested in it. I had two thousand dollars in my savings account, most of which I had had before I came to Washington, so I invested it in the bank. Then it went bankrupt, because of mismanagement. The return from the investment was about two hundred dollars. After that I put my money into annuities and they have paid back.

My sister died in 1934. She had been ill for some time. I could not take care of her and there was no room for a nurse in our apartment, so I finally took her to a sanitarium in Washington where I knew she would have careful attention and be made as comfortable as possible. I then broke up housekeeping, stored my furniture, and took a room at the Allies Inn, downtown near the State Department. I missed the pleasant home life I had had for so long with my sister, but I did not have the heart or the time to try and set up another establishment alone. I was lucky, though, because after a few months my friend Dr. Stella Warner, who worked in the Public

Health Service, asked me to join her in her house in Alexandria. I stayed there for two years and it was a very pleasant interlude. For the first time I had the kind of home life that really got me away from the office. When, after two years, Dr. Warner was assigned to a post in New Mexico we drove out together, taking her two lovely Siamese cats along with us in a basket. On our way we stopped overnight at Ludington, Michigan, where I had stayed and worked when I first came to the United States, but I did not remember it very well. It had been built up so much it was quite different from the days when I was a greenhorn, just learning about my new country.

When I returned to Washington I moved back to the Allies Inn, where I have been ever since. I have a lovely housekeeping apartment, and I hope I shall be able to stay on here indefinitely. Washington is the place where I have my roots and my friends and interests. Except for that, I think I would rather live in San Francisco than any other city I know. I have been in every state except Mississippi and I think I like California about as well as any part of the United States physically. I also like western people. They have much more "go" and ingenuity. The East seems to me to be much more hidebound.

I would not want to live in the country unless I had a family and was very near the city. I would not live alone in the country. I would be scared to death. I have never wanted a house either. In fact, I am not eager for workers to own property as a general thing. It is natural for them to want to own their homes, but I think it may work out to their detriment, because if they own their homes they lose their mobility and are tied down to one job and cannot move away to better themselves. Of course, to own a home makes for a more stable family life, but if you have bought your home and because of that cannot move to a better job and thus improve your standard of living, it does not help much to have a house. There is more to building a family than owning a house. I have seen so many strikes that were terribly hard on the workers because they were afraid of losing the homes they had spent years trying to pay for. The worker does not usually have much money saved. When he buys a house his payments have to be made in such small amounts that it sometimes takes almost a lifetime before the final payment is made. Then, when a couple has skimped for a lifetime to pay for a home, the children have grown up and scattered and built their own homes and all the old people have left is that house. I think renting is better than buying, even though it costs more. It leaves the workers free and that is the most important thing.

27

Irons in the Fire

THE years from 1933 on were very busy ones. It was the beginning of the New Deal. We had first the problems of the National Recovery Administration, then all the relief work and the terrible unemployment, the beginning of the social security program, and the split in the labor movement.

I had known John Lewis for many years and I felt very enthusiastic in the early days of the CIO. I think the CIO started out as a real crusade and many unorganized workers felt that at last they were going to get help. But there were very bitter and tragic feelings among many of the old-line trade unionists who were faced with the decision of whether to stick with their old union if it decided not to go over to the CIO, or to switch to the new group. I have seen some trade unionists actually cry when they had to give up their cards, which they had held almost all their lives, and become members of the new union. In my own case, the International Boot and Shoe Workers Union never affiliated with the CIO, but I really believed in this new method of organization. Women had not had much chance or attention under the American Federation of Labor and I thought that a new day was dawning for them. Although I was a member of the AF of L, I never had any feeling of animosity toward my friends who

were members of the CIO. We were all trade unionists still
and I always felt that if we were going to accomplish anything, we would have to stop making bitter charges against
each other. We had to learn to give and take and work together.

During the early days of the controversy, I remember, one
very amusing episode took place when Margaret Bondfield,
who had been secretary of labor in the British Cabinet, came
over to the United States. Margaret was a very fiery and fear-
less speaker and she was eloquent on the subject of the need
for the two groups to get together. She was a great favorite
with all of us in Washington and shortly before her return
to England we gave a luncheon for her one Sunday afternoon. There were eight or ten of us there and we got talking
about her next visit to the United States and what we would
do to make it possible. Someone remarked that we would
leave no stone unturned to get her back. So we decided to
form what we called the "Stone Turners' Union." A few days
later Margaret gave a tea party at Miss Perkins' house, where
she was staying, and we presented her with credentials for
honorary membership in Local Number 1 of the International
Stone Turners' Union. We also sang her our theme song:

> Oh no! Oh no!
> We're not the CIO
> We never pay du-es
> To John L. Lewis
> Oh no! Oh no!
>
> Oh well, oh well,
> We're not AF of L
> We've never been seen
> With William Green
> Oh well, oh well.
>
> Hi ho! Hi ho!
> We're independent so

We don't give a durn
Whose stones we turn
Hi ho! Hi ho!

Margaret was delighted with this song. She had a lovely contralto voice and she insisted on singing it on every occasion. Just before she was to leave Washington the American Association of University Women gave a big banquet for her. There was an enormous speakers' table stretching the whole length of the Mayflower ballroom, with Margaret in the middle. Hundreds of people had come for the dinner and to hear Margaret speak. Just before the speeches began one of the hotel bellhops came up to the table and presented Margaret with an enormous bunch of red, white, and blue flowers with great streamers of dark blue ribbon on which was lettered in gold "Local Number 1, International Stone Turners' Union." When Margaret saw this she began to laugh so hard she put her head right down on the table. It almost broke up her speech, especially because the two "Stone Turners" who were responsible for this joke placed themselves in the balcony immediately opposite Margaret, and every time she looked up she saw them grinning at her. She would have laughed even harder if she had known that the AF of L man who sat next to me at the speakers' table and the CIO representative who sat next to Elisabeth Christman each got up and walked over to see who had sent the flowers and then came back and asked us in a puzzled way what union that was. They had never heard of it and I think they were worrying about how to get it affiliated with them.

During these years the Women's Bureau had so many irons in the fire it is difficult to sort them all out. One of the problems I always wanted to do something about was the employment conditions of domestic workers.

I had been a domestic worker myself and I was not a success at it, yet it did give me a living until I was able to get started in something else. I have always felt from my own experience that with training and proper standards, domestic work could be made into a respected occupation and not occupy the debased position it does at present. Much more thought must be given to training and standards of employment if we are to get out of the present chaos in domestic employment. I think in a way the employers are getting their training now, when they cannot get people to work for them and have to do the work themselves. In that way they are learning how much there is to do and how long it takes to do it. At the same time, the workers need training too. I think proper training would give dignity to the job instead of putting a domestic worker into a position of servitude. Really, it should be the most dignified occupation we have, because in many cases family life is so dependent on it, but so far no adequate training programs and standards have been set up.

I always felt that we should give more attention to this in the Women's Bureau and that we should collect the facts about this kind of employment, but we never did because we were always prevented from making a study. It was a "hot potato."

One day, when I sat next to Mrs. Roosevelt at lunch, she said, "Mary, you will have to do something about domestic service." I agreed, but I had just talked to Secretary Perkins about it and she had been opposed to our doing anything. While Mrs. Roosevelt was talking I decided that I was not going to take the responsibility for this decision myself, so I asked her to speak to the secretary about it. She agreed and eventually we got the Bureau of the Budget to approve a special appropriation of twenty-five thousand dollars for a study of domestic workers by the Women's Bureau. But when it came up to the Appropriation Committee, the members who were from the South just would not hear of it. It was one of the worst hearings we have ever had. The whole subject got mixed up with the race question, because in Washington and the South most of the domestic workers are Negroes. The southerners did not want to appropriate money for an inves-

tigation that might improve conditions of domestic employment because, they said, the colored people were all right as
they were.

A few days after I appeared before the committee, the secretary talked to them, but they refused to budge and she told
me, "Don't ever bring that up again." So we gave up trying
to get a special appropriation. Instead, whenever we could,
we did bits of research and gathered what information we
could. We worked with other organizations too and tried
to help them, but we never accomplished much.

While we were struggling with the problems of the domestic worker, we also had the question of the Negro woman
industrial worker to deal with and this was even more serious.
The Women's Bureau made several studies of the conditions
under which Negro women were employed and our findings
were really appalling. One of the most serious results of the
low standards for Negro women was a general scaling down
of wages. Just as white women got paid less than white men,
Negro women got many jobs because they would work for
less than white women, and as a result they did not get enough
money to live decently.

I remember once in Birmingham talking to one of the employers who said he could not pay as much as twenty-five
cents an hour to Negroes because if he did they would not
come to work after they had been paid. He said he and other
employers were then paying one dollar for a ten-hour day.
I asked, "When do you pay them?" The reply was, "Every
night we have to pay them one dollar." I said, "Of course they
couldn't live if they weren't paid every day. If they only get
one dollar a day they have to spend it all." He said they would
not come back if they were paid for a whole week at a time,
that they would stay out until the money was gone. I thought
they would come back soon and said, "You know, it has always been said of the workers that if they got more money
they wouldn't work. That's been said for the last century at
least, but that has not been the way it has happened. The

minute there was a way to keep a family in decency, the minute they had food and decent homes, the workers always responded and became real citizens of the country." But he stuck to his opinion, saying, "Those awful niggers wouldn't work." I asked, "Then why do you hire them?" His reply was, "Because we get them for so little." That was just the trouble. It is a vicious circle and it is one that must be broken if the South is to become prosperous.

On the whole I think the South has made tremendous progress during the past ten or fifteen years. This is partly due to the forward-looking program of the federal government during the thirties and the passage of such legislation as the Wage and Hour Law. But it is due also to the gradual development of liberal opinion in the South itself. The First Conference for Human Welfare, which took place in Birmingham, Alabama, in 1938, was the beginning of a very important movement all over the South. It was organized by prominent southerners such as Judge Louise Charlton of Alabama and Frank Graham of North Carolina. Leading southerners in all fields of interest were members of the conference. Its purpose was to focus attention on the problems of the South and to awaken the people there to a sense of responsibility for improving the conditions of the workers.

I was chairman of the section of women in industry at that conference and the Women's Bureau prepared special exhibits showing the part played by women in southern industries and their wages and working conditions. Mrs. Roosevelt came to the conference for one day and made a magnificent speech that night.

When the conference opened we had quite a bit of trouble on account of the Negro issue. The first day went along very well. There were many Negro representatives and they sat with the whites. The meetings had to be held where Negroes were allowed, but there was no segregation.

That evening, Judge Charlton, who was chairman of the conference, and others were called to the mayor's office and told that there had to be segregation at the meetings. The committee protested that it had been a long time since Birmingham had enforced segregation at meetings in the city, although there was a local ordinance to that effect. But the mayor was firm and said the ordinance must be enforced for this meeting because certain citizens had called upon him and insisted on it. In order to hold the meetings at all, therefore, we had to obey the ordinance. Resentment ran high and the delegates, as a whole, did not want to do it. Judge Charlton knew, however, that if there was defiance the meetings would be broken up, and in order not to destroy the unity of the meeting for the purpose it was called for, she begged the delegates to comply. They agreed, but the feeling of resentment was great that evening and the next day.

We were all afraid that when Mrs. Roosevelt arrived she would refuse to speak before a segregated audience. She had never done this before, but when the situation was explained to her, she agreed to make no change in her program. The evening that she was to speak, we were told we should get up there early since by six o'clock a crowd had already begun to assemble outside the hall. It was a huge hall, seating about five thousand people.

Some of us were to sit on the stage with Mrs. Roosevelt and we had a difficult time pushing our way through the crowd. There were thousands left on the outside and before she made her regular speech to the conference, she made a speech to those outside. Inside, all the Negroes were on one side of the hall and all the whites on the other side. It was really a sight from the platform.

Mrs. Roosevelt made a very fine speech, as she usually does — full of everyday common sense, and the crowd went wild about her.

After the conference was over the papers played up the controversy about segregation, but they did not tell of the good things that came out of the conference: the understanding, at least by some, of the special problems in the South that had to be attended to and the minimum standards that should be set up for the working people. In fact, the conference was a focus for the liberal movement in the South, and through the conferences of the same group that have followed from time to time, I think much has been done to educate the people in the South on the need for more progressive action and higher standards of employment for the workers.

One of the leading spirits in the liberal movement of the South has been Mollie Dowd, who is a member of the executive board of the National Women's Trade Union League. She started out as a retail clerk. Known throughout Alabama as "Miss Mollie," she is one of the real characters of the South. She is also one of the most insistent fighters for human liberty and human welfare that I know, never sparing herself in the least and never losing her sense of humor. She always has plenty of stories to tell, but they always have a point that is very refreshing.

One time when the National Women's Trade Union League was holding its convention in Washington, Mrs. Roosevelt invited a number of the delegates to stay with her at the White House. Many of the girls selected for this honor came from the South and Mollie was one of them. They drove up in an old jalopy, to save the cost of railway fare, and when they got to the White House they were much embarrassed because they did not know what to do with their old wreck of a car. Finally one of the White House aides took it away and parked it for them.

While they were at the White House, Mrs. Roosevelt had breakfast with them every morning except once when she was away and the President himself played host. Mollie Dowd with her wonderful stories was a great entertainer on that occasion.

Another problem that we worked very hard on, with more success than we had with standards for domestic workers, was the regulation or abolition of industrial homework. Everyone had known for years of the shocking conditions under which homework was done. The factories sent out work to be done in homes where the sanitary conditions were very bad and where women and children worked terribly long hours for a few cents an hour. The excuse for this was always that the people needed the work, they could not put in a full day's work at the factory, and that by taking work home they were able to get a little extra money. But those of us who knew of the actual conditions were horrified and shocked at this kind of exploitation and we knew, too, that the system was dangerous to public health as well.

The Consumers League was one of the organizations that campaigned against this evil, and some of the unions took it up too, but nothing much was accomplished on a national scale until the days of the National Recovery Administration, when a special committee on homework was set up. The Women's Bureau made a study of conditions under which homework was done and we circulated our findings all over the country. The homework committee of the NRA held any number of hearings and I think they were successful in abolishing homework in some industries. I remember that for the sweater trade in Philadelphia, the committee issued a statement saying that the work should be done in the factory and that if the work was sent into the homes the same wage should be paid as for the work done in the factory. After that, most of the home workers went to the factory to work and when one factory sent out work the women picketed it until the practice was stopped.

Actually there is no effective way to regulate industrial homework. It is impossible to have enough inspectors to see that standards are enforced. That would require one inspector for every home. The only thing to do about homework is to abolish it and to arrange for higher wages for the breadwinner in a family so that his wife and children do not have to supplement the family income by doing homework, or, if there is no regular breadwinner, to provide pensions or relief.

Of course, when the custom of industrial homework is well established in a place, there is nothing to do except try to regulate it. One thing that we advocated and that was tried with fair success was the establishment of workrooms to which the home workers could come for as many hours a day or a week as they could. In these central workrooms the conditions and pay could be regulated. We recommended this for the home industries of Puerto Rico. We sent an agent to study the situation in Puerto Rico and found the most deplorable conditions and ill health among the home workers. A typical case was found in a hut up in the mountains that could be reached only on horseback or on foot. Two sisters were living there. One was in bed with tuberculosis and the other was a cripple. They were trying to keep alive by doing embroidery on the fine handkerchiefs and baby clothes that sold for such high prices in New York. The employers came to Washington to testify before the National Recovery Administration that such people must have that work or they could not live. The trouble was that there was no feeling of civic responsibility for these workers; they were left alone to shift for themselves.

I think that one of the things that helped most in getting better wage standards for the home workers in Puerto Rico was Mrs. Roosevelt's interest. She went down there and rode all over the island seeing what the conditions were. Although homework in Puerto Rico was not abolished, under the National Recovery Administration and later under the federal Wage and Hour Law the rate of pay has been much increased over the two or three cents an hour that was customary.

In the United States, at least in twenty states, homework has been either prohibited by law or regulated to such a degree that it is no longer of great advantage to an employer to use it, because starvation pay is not permitted.

28

Women Workers in World War II

AFTER the passage of the lend-lease legislation in 1941 everyone realized we had to start a tremendous production program if we were really going to be the arsenal of the democracies. I knew, having had the experience of World War I, that women would be called upon to enter every industry and we began urging that women should be given training in the kind of work they would be needed for. On every possible occasion we urged special training facilities for women, but we did not succeed very well because neither the Employment Service nor the Board of Vocational Education wanted to train women. They said that men would be needed first and should be trained first. They did not realize what a shortage of skilled labor was coming and when women went to the Employment Service for training or for jobs they were told there was nothing for them and that they had better forget it. The result was that the women applied for jobs at the factories and they were hired at the gates. In all, I think probably the great majority of women workers added during the war were hired directly by the firms themselves.

It was very interesting to me and a bit disconcerting to find that another generation had grown up knowing practically nothing about the experiences of the last war. This was particularly true among the employers. I always thought it was very strange that when women had been working in factories for generations there should still be employers who did not think they could use women. They thought women would not turn out the work, that they could not work with men, that they could not be disciplined as men were, that the foremen could not handle them. No one seemed to know anything about what women had done in World War I.

I think that was the biggest job for the Women's Bureau during the war — to show employers what women could do and were doing and to advise about standards of employment that would make their work more effective. As soon as the war started we began reporting on where women were being employed and how efficient they were, telling the employers what women could do and what special treatment they needed. This information was at the disposal of all employers and was eagerly accepted. We went into the factories where women were working to see what they were doing and what they could do. We gave that information to other employers in the same industry who had never employed women and were afraid to begin. They would come to us for help and instruction, having found out about us through our reports or from someone who told them to "go to the Women's Bureau."

I spent one whole year doing hardly anything but speaking at management meetings. I remember one of these meetings in New York. There were eight hundred members many of whom had never employed women. One man from an airplane factory said, "I have to employ twenty-one thousand women within the next few months. Before we started hiring them the management got together and talked it all out. We even decided on a uniform, which we thought was very pretty, light blue with white caps, and we thought we'd done a good job. But when we began to employ the women and gave them their uniforms, we realized we had forgotten that we would get fat ones and slim ones. The uniforms were all the same size so that they did not always fit and the women did not want to use them. We called in some of them and asked what was the matter with the uniforms and they said that they didn't want them. They'd rather wear overalls just as the men did. Then we realized that we did not know as much about women as we had thought. It was better to think of them as workers instead of as women."

Of course, showing what women could do was not the whole job. We had to hammer away at standards of employment, just as we had in the last war, if women's work was to be efficient. When we first went into the period of emergency the secretary of labor asked me to formulate standards and policies for the employment of women and I immediately appointed an advisory committee of men and women, representing labor organizations, that met with us in the Women's Bureau. With their cooperation we formulated standards and issued them in a special bulletin that was widely circulated, some hundred thousand copies, during the period of the war. These standards were not very different from the ones we had set up for World War I, except that we included many more provisions for safety in hazardous occupations.

When our standards had finally been set up, the secretary called a meeting of representatives of the War Department, the Navy Department, the War Production Board, and other war emergency organizations. At this meeting we went over the standards again and issued a joint statement, signed by everyone, in regard to policies of employment. This statement incorporated our standards, but added that where it was necessary a dispensation could be given to lengthen hours of work beyond the legal limit, but only for limited periods and after thorough investigation.

We then had a meeting with the state labor commissioners and with representatives of organized labor in order to get their support. They signed the statement, too, and thus began the pattern for employment during the war emergency.

When the War Manpower Commission was set up we went all over this subject again. We had many meetings with members of the commission to discuss standards of employment. They would not accept the standards we had already adopted so we sat around for hours at meeting after meeting, while they worded their standards a little differently from ours, but in the end they were the same.

When the Office of Production Management was set up with William S. Knudsen and Sidney Hillman as cochairmen, I went immediately to Hillman, whom I had known and worked with for more than a quarter of a century, and suggested to him that inasmuch as we knew that women would have to take a great part in war production, it was necessary to appoint a woman to be his adviser on questions affecting women. The first time I spoke to him he agreed that that was a good thing to do and he asked if I would suggest someone for the position. The next time I saw him, however, when I tried to suggest someone, he had changed his mind and said that he had talked it over with the head of his division on training, who thought what they needed was someone to do research. I told him that was not what the Women's Bureau wanted at all, that we wanted a woman to sit in on the actual work of the committee so that she could give advice on both the training and the employment of women. I said, "It is policymaking that we want a woman to be in on." He was not at all agreeable to that, and no woman was ever appointed.

Eventually, after the War Manpower Commission was set up, in response to the urging of many women's organizations, a Woman's Advisory Committee to the commission was appointed, but here again the emphasis was on the "advisory" function and women were not really allowed to have a voice in formulating policies. This was a great disappointment to me and to others who hoped that the time had come when women would be given a real place in determining policies. I was opposed to the formation of the women's committee and cautioned the women's organizations against it. I said what they should do was to insist on having one or two women members on the Labor Advisory Committee. But the Labor

Advisory Committee refused to accept that suggestion and the commission went ahead with plans for the Woman's Advisory Committee.

When I was called in for consultation as to the function of the committee and its membership, the first thing I asked was, "Now, just what is this committee going to be? How will it function with the labor committee? We certainly don't want to create a Woman's Advisory Committee just to sit in the corner." I was told that the chairman of the woman's committee would be a voting member of the Labor Advisory Committee. When I heard that I was satisfied. It was in accord with my original suggestion. But when the Woman's Advisory Committee was finally set up I was surprised and chagrined to find that the chairman was not made a real member of the Labor Advisory Committee. She could attend the meetings and make recommendations but she could not vote. It was a great disappointment. However, in spite of this handicap, the Woman's Advisory Committee did valuable work and was successful in keeping to the fore the need for special consideration of the problems and standards of women's employment. Their publicity was very helpful. I attended most of their meetings, in an advisory capacity, and the Women's Bureau constantly cooperated with them.

One of the great controversies of the war period in respect to women's employment was whether or not a law should be passed requiring registration of women. Some members of the War Manpower Commission urged such a law, but I was opposed to it. In the first place, from the information we got from our agents in many parts of the country, I did not think there was a real shortage of woman labor. Of course, in some localities there was a shortage, but not enough to require registration on a national scale. Chiefly, I thought, the so-called shortage of women was due more to conditions of employment than to lack of labor supply. Women had moved out of the low-paid, traditional woman-employing industries into the higher paid war industries. Then, in the war industries where there was a shortage, I thought that this was due more to unsatisfactory conditions, such as inadequate transportation and poor living quarters, than it was to an actual shortage of workers. We studied many of the emergency war plants and showed the employers how to plan dormitories and recreation facilities so that they could induce women workers to accept employment. In congested areas there was also the problem of arranging women's hours, or otherwise helping them, so that they could get the family shopping done and carry on their family responsibilities at the same time they were doing a day's work in the factory.

All these things came into the problem of the shortage of women workers and I did not think registration was the answer. As an American citizen I do not believe in conscription of workers. I know that the draft was necessary for the armed forces and that it was the only democratic way to build up the fighting force we needed, but I did not think the workers needed to be drafted for industry and I could not see that a national registration law for women was anything more than a first step toward conscription for industry. For this reason I consistently opposed it even though there was heavy pressure for it at certain times. On the whole, however, it got more opposition than support. I received a great deal of correspondence about it, and many delegations came to see me asking my opinion and hoping that I would oppose it. Most of the top people in the administration were opposed, including the War and Navy departments and the President himself. The unions were against it and even the National Chamber of Commerce and the National Manufacturers Association never took definite action on it. But in spite of this, I was rather severely criticized, especially by some women's groups, for not changing my position.

One of our chief difficulties during the war emergency was the number of war agencies that wanted to set up little women's bureaus of their own. Many of the various committees functioning in the government during the war attempted to take on the question of women's employment, but always they had to turn to the Women's Bureau for the facts and figures. We were equipped to give them the information because we had had so many years of experience in collecting it, but I must confess I rather resented a good many attempts that were made by inexperienced newcomers to take over the work of the bureau.

I remember one woman who had been appointed by one of the departments to handle women's employment. She came to see me and I asked her what she was going to do. She answered that she was going to visit plants and suggest standards of work and so forth. I mentioned that I would like to give her copies of our standards, which had been formulated from our own knowledge and experience, but she did not seem to care much about the idea so I did not pursue it. She said she would know better later on what she wanted. She was going to Philadelphia to visit some plants and after she had seen them she would know more about it because she had never been in a plant before. I wanted to ask her how she was going to know what to look for, but I did not. I gave up and let her go. Fortunately, she only lasted a few weeks before she quit. This kind of thing happened a number of times and complicated our job quite a bit, but I suppose it was not such a bad thing in the long run, because at least it showed that more people were recognizing the need for special attention to the problem of women's employment.

All through the war emergency the staff of the bureau was working at top pressure. There seemed to be so much to do and so few of us to do it. We made special studies for other government agencies, such as the War and Navy departments, and much time was spent collecting information for the War Labor Board. In addition to that, we had our agents scattered over all parts of the country, finding out where women were working and under what conditions, advising employers how to use women most effectively, working with the unions to get better terms for women in union contracts.

It was a hectic period, with such great demands and so little money to meet them. Like so many other of the permanent agencies of the government, in time of emergency our appropriation suffered at the expense of the newly created temporary agencies. It was disheartening, but I suppose inevitable, to see the millions appropriated for emergency activities, while we had to plug along on very much the same budgets we had always had. We would scrape up a few thousands here and there for the special work we would do for some of the new projects, but on the whole we had to spread our funds to the limit and there was a great deal that we had to leave undone because we could not hire enough people to do it.

A good deal of our budget trouble came within the department itself. The secretary supported us before the Bureau of the Budget in asking for more money at the beginning of the war emergency, but after that she decided to build up a Working Conditions Service in the Labor Standards Division instead, and told me that she felt the Women's Bureau should not be increased. At one time she stated before the House Appropriations Committee that she was not asking for any additional appropriation for the Women's Bureau, but later on, after there was considerable protest when the report of the hearing was published, she carried the ball for us at the Senate Appropriations Committee hearing and we got an increase of fifty thousand dollars.

The yearly struggle with appropriations was always very wearing and discouraging, but I suppose that is the burden every chief of a government bureau must carry. It is one of the most arduous jobs there is, and one that you have to keep in mind every day of every year you are on the job. I always tried to do the best I could with what I had and hoped that our achievements would earn the increases we needed, but that method was not always as successful as I wanted it to be. Anyway, it was all I could do.

During the latter part of the war I served on a confidential committee appointed by the State Department that was very interesting. We were trying to work up standards on labor conditions and social security that would be used later on at the peace conference. I was appointed chairman of the subcommittee on women. Finally, we issued an excellent report, the substance of which was eventually adopted at the conference of the International Labor Office in Philadelphia in 1944. In this statement were incorporated standards advocating equal pay for women and equal opportunities for them. This was not done without something of a struggle because by this time we had learned the lesson that the simple phrase "Equal Pay for Equal Work" did not mean much when it came to actually applying it. The phraseology that was adopted finally (see page 149) was suggested by us in the Women's Bureau. Now we have an international beginning on getting real equality for women as well as having the movement well under way in the United States. The job is not yet done, but the principle has been accepted internationally, which is a real triumph for all of us who have worked to get it for so many years.

29

Honors and Retirement

EARLY in 1944 when our war program was well under way and most of the policies I thought were essential had been inaugurated, I began to think about retiring. I was tired and discouraged because we could not get enough money to do what I thought we should do and I felt I could not go on much longer appealing to personal friends on Capitol Hill for support. I thought that a new person as head of the bureau might be able to do more than I could.

After twenty-five years in the bureau, I had come to know a great many people all over the United States and I think I had made a good many friends. Three years before, in June 1941, I had been given an honorary degree of doctor of laws at a ceremony at Smith College. This came as a great surprise to me, and I know I never would have received it without the efforts of many good friends who wanted this recognition, not only for me, but for working women as a whole. Mrs. Dwight Morrow, who was a trustee of the college, presented me for the degree and I will never forget my feelings when the beautiful purple and white hood was put around my shoulders and the president of the college, Dr. Herbert Davis, read my citation, which said:

MARY ANDERSON: For 21 years director of the Women's Bureau of the Department of Labor in Washington, who has made herself a leader in the field of industrial relations and devoted her life to improving conditions for working women throughout the country, making use of the knowledge she had acquired by her own experience for 18 years in the garment-making industry and shoe manufacture; a member of the board of the Bryn Mawr summer school for women workers in industry for five years and appointed by the President to represent this country at various international labor conferences in 1933 and 1937; an outstanding public servant and administrator, and largely responsible herself for the valuable research and technical studies undertaken by her Bureau.

I am very proud of that citation, but I do not think it is entirely correct. I did not make myself a leader. If I became a leader it was only because of the support and cooperation of the hundreds of friends and colleagues with whom I had worked for so many years. Mrs. Robins and all the other people who made it possible for me to do what I did are all part of anything I seem to have accomplished. The citation was for them as much as for me, and I accepted it in that spirit. Perhaps the statement that was made in *Life and Labor* by the National Women's Trade Union League will explain better than I can how I felt about this. They said, "When the purple hood was put around her shoulders, we saw Mary in a new setting — a setting that filled us with pride, not only for her, but for the accomplishments of all women workers everywhere."

Just before I was given the honorary degree at Smith, I had had another fine tribute from the General Federation of Women's Clubs. At their golden jubilee celebration in May 1941, the federation presented me with a scroll of honor. They said, among other things, "The paths you have opened [for women in industry] will become broad avenues leading to the goal of social justice, for no one can stop the cavalcade you have started marching onward and upward." Here, too, I think the citation was exaggerated. I did not "start the cavalcade" moving. I have just been one of thousands of others and if I got to the front it was only because there were so many pushing from behind.

And so, after twenty-five years, I came to the decision that it was time for me to step out and make way for someone else. It seemed a good time to quit, because I was sure the secretary of labor would select the right kind of woman to put in my place. I would not have been willing to leave without such an assurance. I talked it over with her and we agreed that Frieda Miller, who had done such distinguished work as labor commissioner of New York State and who was a personal friend of the secretary's, would be ideal for the job. She was not a trade union woman, but I knew that her experience and relations with the trade unions had been extensive and I felt that she would be able to get along with them and at the same time that her contacts in the department were such that she might be more effective than I had been in promoting the bureau. I was much relieved when the secretary finally told me that she had seen Frieda and that she would accept the appointment.

Then I had to face the job of getting out. I called my staff together and told them and there was great consternation. They all seemed very distressed but I am sure they knew it was the right thing for me to do. I planned to retire on the thirtieth of June, but I had one more speech to make before that date. So I went off to Minneapolis on my last official trip, to speak to a crowd of many thousands of people of Swedish descent who were gathered for a celebration of Swedish Day. It was a wonderful experience. I was one of the crowd and it made me proud to realize what a fine part we had all had in our new country. In my speech I told how the Swedish people had come to this country as immigrants, what they had done in different parts of the country: the cooperative movement in Minnesota, their part in the trade union movement, and so on. And I ended my speech with the Swedish word *levnadslust*, which stands for the fine, full life and the zest for living that we want for everyone. Then I came back to Washington and my work was done.

The night before I retired the department gave a banquet in my honor at the Mayflower Hotel. The secretary of labor presided and everyone made a big fuss over me. But it did not seem very real. I kept feeling that all the fine things they said must be about someone else. One thing that was real to me, and that I value most highly, was the letter sent me by President Roosevelt. He said:

DEAR MISS ANDERSON:

I am sorry to learn from the Secretary of Labor that you are leaving the Government service, but I can appreciate your wish to have more leisure time after twenty-five years as head of the Women's Bureau of the United States Department of Labor.

Your work over that quarter of a century has richly earned you the retirement you are taking. You were a pioneer in advocating equal pay for women doing the same work as men and you may well be proud that your ideas as to equal opportunity and equal pay principles were recently incorporated in a recommendation adopted by the International Labor Organization conference in Philadelphia.

Women workers, from the time of World War I, owe much to you for your fine spirit of leadership, your rich common sense, your fidelity to their interests and your successful championship of always practical rights and programs. They, I know, will join with me in well deserved praise of a capable, conscientious and courageous public official who on retiring to private life leaves a monument of constructive achievement in the best interest of millions of women wage earners. I want to thank you, in their behalf, as well as my own for the great services you have rendered your country so unselfishly.

I hope that even in retirement your Government may continue to call upon you for advice and help when problems affecting women workers arise.

Sincerely yours,
FRANKLIN D. ROOSEVELT

The next day was my last in the office. The work went as usual in the morning, but for lunch my entire staff gathered in the little dining room in the department and we reminisced about the old days. They gave me a beautiful bracelet and pin as a memento of our years together and then we all said good-by. It was a great emotional trial. I did not go back to the office after that day. I just went home and left Washington the next day for a short vacation.

But I did not rest for long. I did not leave the bureau with the intention of quitting work. I wanted to work with the women's organizations I had always been a member of. I wanted to do what I could for the same causes I had worked for in the bureau, and it has turned out that way. I am much freer now and of course I have accumulated through the years much information and experience that can be useful. I go on the same way, but at my own pace.

Almost the first thing I did after I quit was to attend the Democratic National Convention to speak against the endorsement of the equal rights amendment in the party platform. Now, among other things, I am working for a federal law requiring equal pay for women. We think this has a fair chance of success. After we get that I know there will be something more to do to help improve conditions and opportunities for women. As long as I am able to I shall keep on. I still have a zest for living and I know that I have had a fine, full life.

Index